Family Bible Study

THE
Herschel
HOBBS
COMMENTARY

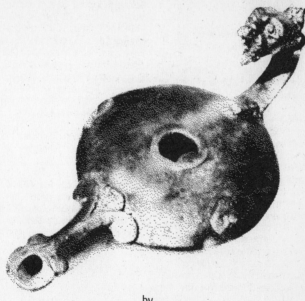

by

Robert J. Dean

FALL 2001
Volume 2, Number 1

ROSS H. McLAREN
Biblical Studies Specialist

Carolyn Gregory
Production Specialist

Stephen Smith
Graphic Designer

Frankie Churchwell
Technical Specialist

Send questions/comments to
  Ross H. McLaren, editor
  127 9th Ave., North
  Nashville, TN 37234-0175
  Email: HHobbsComm@lifeway.com

Management Personnel

Louis B. Hanks, *Acting Director*
Adult Sunday School Ministry Department
Louis B. Hanks, *Associate Director*
Sunday School Group
BILL L. TAYLOR, *Director*
Sunday School Group

ACKNOWLEDGMENTS.–We believe the Bible has God for its author; salvation for its end; and truth, without any mixture of error, for its matter and that all Scripture is totally true and trustworthy. The 2000 statement of *The Baptist Faith and Message* is our doctrinal guideline.

Unless otherwise indicated, all Scripture quotations are from the *King James Version*. This translation is available in a Holman Bible and can be ordered through LifeWay Christian Stores. Scripture quotations identified as CEV are from the *Contemporary English Version*. Copyright © American Bible Society 1991, 1992. Used by permission. Quotations marked HCSB are from the *Holman Christian Standard Bible: Experiencing the Word Through the Gospels*. Copyright © Broadman & Holman Publishers 1999. Used by permission. Excerpts from *The Jerusalem Bible*, copyright © 1966 by Darton, Longman and Todd, Ltd., and Doubleday and Company, Inc. Used by permission of the publisher. Passages marked NASB are from the *New American Standard Bible: 1995 Update*. © The Lockman Foundation, 1960, 1962, 1963, 1968, 1971, 1972, 1973, 1975, 1977, 1995. Used by permission. This translation is available in a Holman Bible and can be ordered through Lifeway Christian Stores. Quotations marked NEB are from *The New English Bible*. Copyright © The Delegates of the Oxford University Press and the Syndics of the Cambridge University Press, 1961, 1970. Reprinted by permission. Quotations marked NIV are from the *Holy Bible, New International Version*, copyright © 1973, 1978, 1984 by International Bible Society (NIVmg. = NIV margin). This translation is available in a Holman Bible and can be ordered through Lifeway Christian Stores. Quotations marked NKJV are from the *New King James Version*. Copyright © 1979, 1980, 1982. Thomas Nelson, Inc., Publishers. Reprinted with permission. This translation is available in a Holman Bible and can be ordered through Lifeway Christian Stores. Quotations marked NRSV are from the *New Revised Standard Version of the Bible*, copyright © 1989 by the Division of Christian Education of the National Council of the Churches of Christ in the United States of America. Used by permission. All rights reserved. Quotations marked REB are from *The Revised English Bible*. Copyright © Oxford University Press and Cambridge University Press, 1989. Reprinted by permission.

The Herschel Hobbs Commentary (ISSN 0191-4219), *Family Bible Study*, is published quarterly for adult teachers and members using the Family Bible Study series by LifeWay Christian Resources of the Southern Baptist Convention, 127 Ninth Avenue, North, Nashville, Tennessee 37234, Gene Mims, President, LifeWay Church Resources, a division of LifeWay Christian Resources; James T. Draper, Jr., President, Ted Warren, Executive Vice-President, LifeWay Christian Resources; Bill L. Taylor, Director, Sunday School Group. © Copyright 2001 LifeWay Christian Resources of the Southern Baptist Convention. All rights reserved. Single subscription to individual address, $20.95 per year. If you need help with an order, WRITE LifeWay Church Resources Customer Service, 127 Ninth Avenue North, Nashville, Tennessee 37234-0113; For subscriptions, FAX (615) 251-5818 or EMAIL subscribe@lifeway.com. For bulk shipments mailed quarterly to one address, FAX (615) 251-5933 or EMAIL CustomerService@lifeway.com. Order ONLINE at www.lifeway.com. Mail address changes to: *The Herschel Hobbs Commentary, Family Bible Study*, 127 Ninth Avenue, North, Nashville, TN 37234-0113.

Dedicated to the Memory of

Dr. Baker James Cauthen,

1909-1985

Missionary to China, 1939-1953

Executive Director, Foreign Mission Board, 1954-1979,

Who called an entire generation to consider missions.

Contents

Study Theme

Joshua: Model of Obedience   6

Study Theme

God's Plan for Families   56

Contents

Study Theme

Telling the Lost about Jesus   96

Study Theme

Joshua: Model of Obedience

Joshua was a remarkable man. He was an aide to Moses. He was later chosen to lead the Israelites following the death of Moses. Just as Moses was suited to his calling, Joshua was suited to his. For one thing, Joshua was a military leader. But most important of all, he was a man of faith, courage, and obedience to the Lord. Something is said of Joshua that is said of very few leaders. The Lord used Joshua's faith and obedience to influence not only the people of his own generation but also of the next generation.

In this five-session unit on Joshua the biblical content will be passages about Joshua, and these will be studied to explore the importance of the kind of faith that is expressed in obedience to God. Based on passages from the Book of Numbers and the Book of Joshua, these lessons will focus on Joshua as a biblical role model of the obedient life. The studies begin with the faith and obedience of Joshua when he and Caleb were the only ones of the 12 spies who pleaded with the unbelieving people to enter the promised land. Then comes a lesson on the Lord's call for Joshua to succeed Moses as leader and to lead Israel into the promised land. The third lesson is based on the biblical account of the Israelites crossing the Jordan River while the Lord held back the waters of the flooded river. The fourth lesson is the story of the fall of the city of Jericho. The fifth lesson focuses on Joshua's final call for faith and obedience.

This study is designed to help you—

• obey God because He is worthy of your trust and obedience (Sept. 2)

• consistently follow leaders who reflect God's character (Sept. 9)

• leave a legacy of obedience to God (Sept. 16)

• obey God completely, even if you don't understand all the reasons for His commands (Sept. 23)

• serve the Lord above all others (Sept. 30)

Who are your favorite Bible heroes? Why? _____

_____

How are these people different from you? _____

Affirming God's Worthiness

Background Passage: Numbers 13:1–14:45
Focal Passage: Numbers 13:1-2; 14:6-9,26-30,36-38
Key Verses: Numbers 14:8-9

❖ *Significance of the Lesson*

• The *Theme* of this lesson is God is worthy of our trust and expects our obedience.
• The *Life Question* this lesson seeks to address is, Why should I trust God enough to obey Him?
• The *Biblical Truth* is that God is worthy of our trust and obedience.
• The *Life Impact* is to help you obey God because He is worthy of your trust and obedience.

Trusting and Obeying God

In secular worldviews, God, if viewed as existing at all, is seen as distant, uninvolved, and unconcerned with people's lives. Understanding and obeying God's will are not factors in such lifestyles.

In the biblical worldview, however, God is in control of history and personally involved in people's lives. He is all knowing and all powerful. His self-giving love seeks the best for His people. Therefore, He is worthy of our trust and expects our obedience.

Decision at Kadesh Barnea

Israel's arrival at Kadesh Barnea was a decisive time for the people whom God had delivered from slavery in Egypt and with whom He had entered into a covenant. God had promised Abraham, Isaac, and Jacob that their descendants would receive Canaan as their own land. At Kadesh Barnea, they had the opportunity to claim that promise. However, Israel made a foolish decision and failed to claim God's promise. Their bad decision doomed the adult generation to wander for 40 years in the wilderness until all over the age of 20 (except Joshua and Caleb) died.

Joshua's Earlier Life

Joshua is first mentioned in Exodus 17, when shortly after leaving Egypt, he led the fighting men of Israel against the Amalekites. He became a servant of Moses and went with him part of the way up Mount Sinai (Ex. 24:13). He was with Moses when they came down to find the people worshiping a golden calf (32:17). He was with Moses at the tabernacle (33:11). He was selected as the leader from his tribe of Ephraim who would be one of those who explored Canaan (Num. 13:8). His name was changed by Moses from "Oshea" (KJV) or "Hoshea" (NIV, NKJV) to "Jehoshea" (KJV) or "Joshua" (NIV, NKJV; Num. 13:16). *Hoshea* means "deliverance" or "salvation." *Joshua* means "the Lord saves." This is the Hebrew version of "Jesus."

Word Study: *Murmur, murmurings*

The root of the Hebrew word translated **murmur** and **murmurings** is *lun*. The word means to "murmur," "grumble," or "complain." This word is found only in Exodus 15–17; Numbers 14; 16–17; and Joshua 9:18. In Numbers 14 it is found in verses 2,27,29, and 36. It is used only in reference to specific complains in the wilderness.

❖ *Search the Scriptures*

God instructed the Israelites to send out one leader from each of the twelve tribes, with the assignment to explore the land of Canaan, which God wanted to give to Israel. When the majority reported that the people in Canaan were too strong for the Israelites to conquer, the Israelites rebelled against Moses and God. Only Joshua and Caleb stood and called the people to trust and obey God. God punished the rebellious people by denying them entry into Canaan, but He promised that Joshua and Caleb would live to enter the promised land.

God Gives Instruction (Num. 13:1-2)

What did God instruct the people to do? Why did God ask that a leader from each tribe form the group? How do verses 17-20 enlarge on the spies' mission? How did God intend to give Israel the land? Why are leaders so important?

13:1-2: And the LORD spake unto Moses, saying, ²Send thou men, that they may search the land of Canaan, which I give unto the children of Israel: of every tribe of their fathers shall ye send a man, everyone a ruler among them.

The Lord told Moses what to tell the people. They were told to **send** a group of 12 men into **the land of Canaan,** one from each of the tribes. Deuteronomy 1:21-23 records that the people had asked for a group of men to go through Canaan before the others entered. Numbers 13:1-2 reveals that God Himself told Moses to instruct the people to proceed with this plan. Each **man** was to be **a ruler** ("leader," NIV) in his **tribe.** These names differ from the list of leaders in Numbers 1:5-15. Perhaps leaders who were appropriate for tasks in 1:5-15 were not the best ones to undertake a different task. The names of only two of these spies are mentioned after the list in 13:4-15—Joshua and Caleb. The age of the leaders may have been a factor. Only younger men were able to make such a long survey of the land. Joshua is called "a young man" in Exodus 33:11. Caleb was 40 when the 12 spies were sent out (Josh. 14:7).

Their mission was to **search the land of Canaan. Search** ("explore," NIV) is the Hebrew word *tur,* which is sometimes translated "spy out" (NASB, NKJV). The *King James Version* has a form of **search** in most of the uses of this word in chapters 13–14; however, in 13:16,17 it uses "spy out." We often refer to these men as spies. However, according to Walter Riggans, the Hebrew word *tur* "really does not talk about 'spies' or 'spying,' as we can see in the NEB's translation of the verb by 'to explore' or the Jerusalem Bible's translation by 'to make a reconnaissance.' The fact is that God is inviting the tribes to see for themselves via representatives who are considered responsible, how wonderful the land is that God has prepared for them."[1]

Their mission is spelled out more completely in 13:17-20. The emphasis was on looking for the positives about the land, but the Israelites were told to note also such things as the size of the people and their fortifications. Thus the idea in the word *tur* may be on exploring, not spying; however, their assignment did include some information that would be helpful when they sought to conquer the land.

These verses, when read in light of later actions by the spies, underscore the importance of God's people having good leaders. At the top of the list of qualifications should be faith in God and obedience to Him. This applies to pastors, deacons, Sunday School leaders, and so forth. Leaders have influence, and it can be for bad or for good.

Verses 21-25 summarize the spies' trip throughout Canaan. As Moses had requested, they brought back a cluster of grapes that two men had to carry on a pole between them. When the 12 men returned to give their report, it soon became apparent that there was a majority report and a minority report. Both groups agreed that the land flowed "with milk and honey" (13:26-27). However, 10 of the 12 focused on the strength of the people and their fortifications (vv. 28-29). Caleb spoke for himself and Joshua by saying, "Let us go up at once, and possess it; for we are well able to overcome it" (v. 30). The others strongly disagreed. They spoke of the inhabitants of the land as giants, before whom the Israelites were like grasshoppers (vv. 31-33).

The word **give** is important. God had promised that Canaan was a good land and that He intended to give the Israelites this land. Moses assumed that the spies were not asked to recommend whether to enter Canaan, but how to go about it. Ten of the spies apparently thought they could recommend not entering Canaan—and did.

God Promises Blessing (Num. 14:6-9)

What was the situation when Joshua and Caleb spoke out in 14:6-9? Why did Joshua not speak up earlier? Against what sins did they warn? What challenges did they make? What promises did they reinforce? What were the differences in Joshua's and Caleb's view about God compared to the view of the other spies?

14:6-9: And Joshua the son of Nun, and Caleb the son of Jephunneh, which were of them that searched the land, rent their clothes: ⁷and they spake unto all the company of the children of Israel, saying, The land, which we passed through to search it, is an exceeding good land. ⁸If the LORD delight in us, then he will bring us into this land, and give it us; a land which floweth with milk and honey. ⁹Only rebel not ye against the LORD, neither fear ye the people of the land; for they are bread for us: their defense is departed from them, and the LORD is with us: fear them not.

The immediate background to 14:6-9 is in verses 1-5. The evil report of the 10 spies was enough to arouse the worst in the people. They cried out and wept all night (v. 1). They "murmured against Moses and against Aaron" (v. 2). They said they would have been better off if they had died in Egypt. They even said they wished they had died in the wilderness. Then they accused the Lord of bringing them into the wilderness and sending them into Canaan so the adults would be killed and their children would be enslaved by the Canaanites. They said they ought to return to Egypt. And they were about to appoint a new leader to take them back to Egypt.

They had made the same complaint before. Shortly after being delivered at the Red Sea, the Israelites complained, "Would to God we had died by the hand of the Lord in the land of Egypt, when we sat by the fleshpots, and when we did eat bread to the full; for ye have brought us forth into this wilderness, to kill this whole assembly with hunger" (Ex. 16:3). Stunned by this reaction, Moses and Aaron fell down on their faces (14:5).

Joshua and **Caleb** had been among **them that searched** out **the land.** However, they drew different conclusions from what they saw in Canaan, especially when they remembered God's promises. Caleb already had delivered a brief report in Numbers 13:30. Now it became apparent that only he and Joshua of the spies shared this view. We wonder why Joshua had not spoken up earlier. Timothy R. Ashley explained: "From the point of view of the whole text as it stands, it makes sense for Joshua to have kept silent until this point. Before this point the dispute had simply been over whether the land was conquerable. God's leadership had only tacitly been involved. Caleb had expressed the positive point of view well enough without the need for additions from Joshua (or Moses, for that matter). But in 14:1-4 the people had responded in a way that challenged not only the human leadership but also the divine leadership."[2]

Joshua and Caleb **rent** ("tore," NIV) **their clothes,** a common way of showing deep grief. The people also had grieved and wept; however, the people's grief was sorrow that grew out of their fear and unbelief. These two men shared the deep concern of Moses and Aaron. They expressed their concern in what they said to the people. First of all, they stressed what even the others had admitted—**the land, which we passed through to search it, is an exceeding good land.** God had promised that it would be. Therefore, the other spies ought to have realized that if God was right about the goodness of the land, He also could be trusted in what He said about their ability to take the land.

God had promised to give the land of Canaan to the descendants of Abraham, Isaac, and Jacob. This would be done because God promised it, but God did not promise to give it to any generation of Israelites who acted as they had. Joshua and Caleb spoke as members of the generation that had been delivered from Egypt. God had promised them, **If the Lord delight in** ("is pleased with," NIV) **us, then he will bring us into this land.** The word **if** shows that entering the land was conditioned on their faith and obedience. If they acted with courageous faith and obedience, God would **bring** them **into this land, and give it** to them. The land is described, as it so often is in the Old Testament, as **a land which floweth with milk and honey.** This signified a rich and bountiful land. Goats' milk would be plentiful, and the honey of bees would abound.

Verse 9 emphasizes the certainty that the Lord could give them the land if they went forward with courageous faith. The two spies warned the people about two sins they were committing: One was stated like this: **rebel not ye against the Lord. Rebel** translates *marad*, which means to revolt or flagrantly disobey a recognized authority. Rebellion against God is the worst kind of rebelling. The Lord does not take this sin lightly—as we see in the fate of the rebels.

The second warning was not to **fear.** The report of the 10 spies reeked of fear that the inhabitants would defeat them. Joshua and Caleb gave two vivid descriptions of why they should trust and obey the Lord without fear of their enemies. **They are bread for us** meant that the Israelites with God's help would have no more trouble taking Canaan than they would in eating bread. The 10 spies had said that the land of Canaan "eateth up the inhabitants thereof" (13:32). Joshua and Caleb turned that figure around and said that the Israelites would do the eating.

Defense ("protection," NIV) is the word for "shadow" or "shade." "In the hot and arid regions of the Middle East, the notion of a shadow or shade is a symbol of grace and mercy, a relief from the searing heat (cf. Ps 91:1). Sometimes the wings of a mother bird form the shadow of protection for her young; in the imagery of the poets of Israel, this mother-hen language is used of the protective care of God (e.g., Ps 17:8). God has served as a protecting shadow for the peoples of the land of Canaan; now that protection is gone."[3] They have no divine protection, but Israel does.

The main reason for Joshua's and Caleb's confidence was expressed like this: **The Lord is with us: fear them not.** The assurance that God is with us is the basis for courageous faith and complete obedience. God had shown in the past what He could do in the midst of His people; now they should trust Him and act in obedience.

How can two people or two groups of people see the same things and reach contradictory conclusions? All 12 of the spies had seen the same things in Canaan, but one group recommended not entering and Joshua and Caleb recommended going. Here are two different views of God. True followers believe God loves them and that He is able to care for them. The other response is based on the view that God does not love them and He is unable to help them.

God Expects Obedience (Num. 14:26-29,36-37)

Why did the Israelites grumble so much? What does grumbling reveal about a person? In what sense did God give them what they asked for?

14:26-29: And the LORD spake unto Moses and unto Aaron, saying, ²⁷How long shall I bear with this evil congregation, which murmur against me? I have heard the murmurings of the children of Israel, which they murmur against me. ²⁸Say unto them, As truly as I live, saith the LORD, as ye have spoken in mine ears, so will I do to you: ²⁹Your carcasses shall fall in this wilderness; and all that were numbered of you, according to your whole number, from twenty years old and upward, which have murmured against me.

Unfortunately, the mob of rebellious Israelites responded to the words of Joshua and Caleb by preparing to stone them to death (v. 10). The Lord asked Moses how much of this did He have to hear before He gave up on Israel. He equated their grumbling with a lack of faith. He told Moses that He could destroy these people and make a new start with Moses and his family (vv. 11-12). Moses then interceded for the people—much as he had after they had made the golden calf (vv. 13-19; Ex. 33). He ended the prayer by citing what God had revealed to him after the earlier intercession (compare vv. 18-19 with Ex. 34:6-7). God promised to pardon the people, but He pronounced judgment on the people. They would never see the promised land, but Caleb would (vv. 20-25).

The LORD asked **how long** He would have to listen to **this evil congregation** ("wicked community," NIV) **murmur** ("complain," NKJV; "grumble," NIV) **against** Him. He said He had **heard the murmurings of the children of Israel, which they murmur against me.** In the short time since they left Egypt, the people had grumbled repeatedly against Moses; however, such grumblings ultimately were against God.

God pronounced judgment on these grumblers. Ironically, He told them, **As ye have spoken in mine ears, so will I do to you.** Read

Numbers 14:1-4 again, especially verse 3. They complained that they would have been better off if they died in the wilderness than to be defeated launching an unsuccessful attack on Canaan. So God said, "I will give you exactly what you wanted" (CEV). They had asked to die in the wilderness, and God said that He would give them what they had asked for. Speaking to the adults, God said, **Your carcasses shall fall in this wilderness.** Apparently the grumbling in 14:1-4 included the entire adult generation, for God condemned all who were **from twenty years old and upward, which have murmured against me.** The adult generation, which had come out of Egypt, would never enter the promised land; they would die during 40 years of wandering in the wilderness (v. 34).

The Israelites had complained that if they invaded Canaan, their children would be a prey for the enemy. God told them that only their children would ever see the promised land. When they grew up, they would claim the promise of the land by their trust and obedience (v. 31). But before that happened, the adult generation would have wandered in the wilderness and died (vv. 32-35).

14:36-37: **And the men, which Moses sent to search the land, who returned, and made all the congregation to murmur against him, by bringing up a slander upon the land, [37]even those men that did bring up the evil report upon the land, died by the plague before the LORD.**

What about the 10 spies who brought the evil report? They had been the evil influence that led the people **to murmur against God.** They had brought **a slander upon** ("spreading a bad report about," NIV) **the land.** Their punishment was immediate and final: They **died by the plague before the LORD.**

God promised the blessing of receiving the land of milk and honey, but receiving this promise called for faith and obedience, which most of the Israelites did not have. Instead of trusting and obeying God, they responded to the promise with grumbling, rebellion, and fear. We more easily recognize the dangers of rebellion and fear than we do the danger of grumbling. Our grumbling is against the Lord. Paul was thinking of Israel's history of grumbling when he wrote to Christians not to follow the bad example of these grumbling Israelites (1 Cor. 10:10). He wrote to the Philippians, "Do all things without murmurings and disputings" (Phil. 2:14).

A father had just said the blessing before he and his family ate breakfast. Then he began to complain about hard times and about the food itself. His little daughter had heard all this. She asked him,

"Daddy, do you suppose God heard wh~

Her father thought she was referr~
tainly," he replied, thinking he coul~

"And did He hear what you said ~
The father's reply was, "Of course."

"Then, Daddy, which does God believe?"

Persistent complaining is the opposite of trus~
God's good gifts, and contentment with what He gi~
blessings to people of faith who face difficulties with fa~

God Rewards Faithfulness (Num. 14:30,38)

What qualities did Joshua and Caleb have? How did God reward them.

14:30,38: Doubtless ye shall not come into the land, concerning which I sware to make you dwell therein, save Caleb the son of Jephunneh, and Joshua the son of Nun. . . . [38]But Joshua the son of Nun, and Caleb the son of Jephunneh, which were of the men that went to search the land, lived still.

Only two adults of the generation that came out of Egypt entered the promised land: **Caleb** and **Joshua.** What God said about Caleb in verse 24 was also true of Joshua. God said of Caleb that he "followed me fully" ("wholeheartedly," NIV).

What qualities did these two men display in Numbers 13–14? They had leadership qualities and fulfilled their responsibilities to God and to Israel. They remembered what God had done in the past, and thus believed that He was trustworthy when He told them to enter Canaan. They took a bold stand for God when nearly everyone was against them. They warned the people against rebelling against God and being so afraid of the enemy that they refused to trust and obey God.

In other words, they acted in the opposite way from the people. The people refused to trust God; Joshua and Caleb trusted Him. The people feared the giants; Joshua and Caleb acted with courage. The people grumbled against God; Joshua and Caleb testified for God. The people rebelled against God; Joshua and Caleb obeyed the Lord.

The people finally realized their foolish actions in failing to enter Canaan. They planned to launch an attack on Canaan. Moses warned them that if they tried to do this, the Lord would not be with them. They ignored this warning, launched an attack, and were utterly defeated (vv. 39-45). They were too late in their response.

adult generation had died, Joshua and Caleb showed the
th and obedience they advocated in Numbers 14:9. There
giants in the land and the cities were still well fortified; but
ua and Caleb led a new generation into the land, God gave
the victory. As we look ahead in their lives, we see Joshua trust-
nd obeying God when they crossed the Jordan River and captured
cho and eventually all of Canaan. He became a highly respected
ader in every area of his life. Caleb appeared before Joshua when he
was 85 years old; he had come to claim his part of the land, even
though some of the giants were in the land he had been promised.
Caleb acted with faith, courage, and obedience and claimed his portion
of the promised land (Josh. 14:6-15).

❖ *Spiritual Transformations*

When the Israelites arrived at the border of the promised land, God
told them to send out 12 spies—each one a leader in his tribe—to explore the land as preparation for entering. When 10 spies gave an evil
report and the people rebelled, Joshua and Caleb stood boldly for
going into Canaan. The rebellious adult generation was condemned to
die while wandering in the wilderness, and the 10 spies died right
away. Of the adult generation that came out of Egypt, only Joshua and
Caleb entered the promised land.

What does it mean to be trustworthy? This is a quality of someone
who in the past has kept promises and proved dependable. The people of faith in the Bible believed God is trustworthy because He had
delivered them and blessed them in the past. He had kept past
promises; therefore, they believed He would keep future promises.
They trusted and obeyed the trustworthy God.

*How has God shown Himself trustworthy in your life?*_____

*How have you responded to His trustworthiness?*_____

Prayer of Commitment: Lord, thank You for being trustworthy;
help me to trust and obey You.

[1]Walter Riggans, *Numbers,* in The Daily Study Bible Series [Philadelphia: The Westminster Press, 1983], 106.

[2]Timothy R. Ashley, *The Book of Numbers,* in The New International Commentary on the Old Testament [Grand Rapids: William B. Eerdmans Publishing Company, 1993], 248.

[3]Ronald B. Allen, *Numbers,* in the Expositor's Bible Commentary, vol. 2 [Grand Rapids: Zondervan Publishing House, 1990], 816.

[4]Leslie B. Flynn, *Did I Say That?* [Nashville: Broadman Press, 1959], 98.

Following Godly Leaders

Background Passage: Numbers 27:15-23; Joshua 1:1-18
Focal Passage: Numbers 27:15-20; Joshua 1:1-3,5-9,16-17
Key Verse: Joshua 1:9

❖ *Significance of the Lesson*

• The *Theme* of this lesson is God wants His people to follow godly leaders.

• The *Life Question* this lesson seeks to address is, What kind of leader does God want me to follow.

• The *Biblical Truth* is that God has established leadership for His people and He wants them to follow leaders who reflect His character.

• The *Life Impact* is to help you consistently follow leaders who reflect God's character.

Views on Leaders

In secular worldviews, people tend to follow leaders who have the world's standard of success, who are popular, and who follow the world's way of thinking. In secular worldviews, a leader's character is for the most part unimportant.

In the biblical worldview, God has established standards of leadership for His people. God wants His people to follow godly leaders whom He has called and who have such characteristics as servanthood, courage, obedience to God, and trustworthiness.

A Leadership Crisis

Moses had provided human leadership for many years through many crises. He was the human leader whom God used to deliver Israel from slavery in Egypt. He led them through the Red Sea. He led them to Sinai and mediated God's covenant at Mount Sinai. He tried to lead them into the promised land at Kadesh Barnea. He was with them during the years in the wilderness. However, God had told Moses that he would die before the people entered into Canaan. Thus Israel faced a crisis in finding a new leader who was God's choice to lead the people across the Jordan River and lead them to be victorious in conquering the land of Canaan.

Applying This Lesson to Life

This week's lesson focuses on the need to follow godly leaders. The Bible passages apply to how a church calls a pastor, deacons, Sunday School teachers, and other leaders. It guides leaders and potential leaders in being the kind of leaders God's Word teaches. And it shows how followers should support godly leaders and how each one should act in areas in which they are leaders. One word of caution: Do not let this session become a gripe session about a church leader. The temptation in this lesson may be to use it as a basis for judging and criticizing church leaders.

Word Study: *Minister*

The word *m^{e}sharet* is translated "minister" in Joshua 1:1. It also may be translated "aide" (NIV) or "assistant" (NKJV). It is a different word from "servant," which is used to describe Moses in the same verse. *M^{e}sharet* is also used of Joshua in Exodus 24:13; 33:11; and Numbers 11:28.

❖ *Search the Scriptures*

God gave Moses instructions about preparing Joshua to be Israel's next leader and presenting him to the people as their next leader. Both Moses and Joshua were servants. God told Joshua not to be afraid but courageous because God was with him. He promised success to Joshua if he obeyed the law. A group of Israelites promised to follow Joshua as they had Moses.

Spiritual Authority for Leadership (Num. 27:15-20)

When and why did Moses pray for God to name a new leader to succeed Moses? What qualities did Moses ask that the new leader have? Why did God name Joshua? What did God tell Moses to do to set

Joshua apart as his successor? How did Joshua reflect principles of spiritual authority for leadership?

Numbers 27:15-17: And Moses spake unto the LORD, saying, ¹⁶Let the LORD, the God of the spirits of all flesh, set a man over the congregation, ¹⁷which may go out before them, and which may go in before them, and which may lead them out, and which may bring them in; that the congregation of the LORD be not as sheep which have no shepherd.

The setting for this passage is after the Lord had told Moses that he would not be allowed to enter the promised land. Numbers 20:1-13 tells how Moses failed to obey the Lord completely when he was provoked once again by the people's complaints. He would be allowed to see the promised land from a distance, but he would not enter it. Thus the narrative in Numbers 27:15-20 occurred near the end of Moses' life and shortly before the Israelites entered the promised land. Moses had wanted to lead them on this final step, but he was told that someone else would do it.

Moses spake unto the LORD. In other words, the first thing Moses did was to ask God to show who the next leader would be. Moses did not choose his successor, nor did the people select him. Instead, God named him. This points up the first principle for seeking godly leaders. We must pray for the Lord to lead the people of God to a leader whom God wants for a specific task. In Baptist churches, the church approves a person as pastor. The pastor search committee and the church must bathe every step of the process with prayer.

Moses used a rare title for **the LORD.** He called Him **the God of the spirits of all flesh.** The only other use of this title is in Numbers 16:22. The title recognizes the sovereignty of God over all people. It emphasizes His concern for the spiritual welfare of His people. Moses asked God to **set** ("appoint," NIV) **a man over the congregation.**

The new leader needed to be able to **go out before them** and **go in before them.** He also needed to be able to **lead them out** and **bring them in.** The first pair probably is a reference to his leadership in battle. The other may reflect his role as shepherd of the flock. Supporting this view is the last part of verse 17: **that the congregation of the LORD be not as sheep which have no shepherd.** Leaders often were compared to shepherds. They were to care for, lead, defend, and feed their flock. Ezekiel compared the people of his day to sheep without a shepherd (34:1-6). Many claimed to be shepherds, but many were unworthy of the title. Jesus saw the multitudes as sheep without a shepherd (Matt. 9:36). As in Ezekiel's day, there were many would-be shepherds, but they neglected true care for their people.

Numbers 27:18-20: And the Lord said unto Moses, Take thee Joshua the son of Nun, a man in whom is the spirit, and lay thine hand upon him; ¹⁹and set him before Eleazar the priest, and before all the congregation; and give him a charge in their sight. ²⁰And thou shalt put some of thine honor upon him, that all the congregation of the children of Israel may be obedient.

The Lord named **Joshua the son of Nun** as the next leader. **Joshua** was **a man in whom is the spirit.** Was this God's Spirit or the human spirit of a good man? Some translations, such as the *King James Version* and the *New International Version,* do not capitalize **spirit,** but others do (NKJV; NASB). The Old Testament does not emphasize the Spirit of God in the way done in the New Testament. In the New Testament, however, a definite quality of Christian leaders is to be filled with the Spirit.

God told Moses to do several things to present Joshua as his successor. First, he was told, **lay thine hand upon him.** The practice of laying on of hands continued in the New Testament (Acts 6:6; 13:3; 1 Tim. 4:14; 2 Tim. 1:6). This signifies divine choice and the Spirit on the person.

Second, Moses was told to **set him before Eleazar the priest.** Aaron had been the high priest until his death. Eleazar was named as his successor (Num. 20:28). During his lifetime, Moses himself was a priest who stood before God. Joshua, who was not from the tribe of Levi, would count on Eleazar to perform the priestly roles. This does not mean that Joshua was not a deeply spiritual leader, for he was; however, he never had the face-to-face relation with God that Moses had. Setting Joshua before the high priest was another way of declaring him to be God's chosen leader. Third, Joshua was also to be **set . . . before all the congregation.** At the same time, Moses was told to **give him a charge in their sight** ("commission him in their presence," NIV). These actions would ensure that everyone understood that God had named him to be their new leader.

Honor, in verse 20, is found here for the first time in the Old Testament. "Elsewhere the word is used of the 'honor' or 'majesty' due to God or a king. . . . Most English translations have settled for 'authority,' since the purpose is that the people of the congregation *might obey.*"[1] The people were to **be obedient** to the Lord and to His chosen leader. Of course, people of faith are obedient to God and His Word. Insofar as the leader is true to God and His Word, believers are to follow a God-called leader as he leads them to obey the Word.

A new leader will not be just like the old leader. No two people are just alike. Thus a new leader is not called to replace the former leader but to use his own talents in fulfilling God's call. When Thomas Jefferson presented his credentials as the United States Minister to France, the French premier said, "I see that you have come to replace Benjamin Franklin," who had been very popular with the French. Jefferson wisely replied, "I have come to succeed him. No one can replace him."[2] Joshua was not called to be Moses but to be himself and to do what he had been called to do.

Servanthood (Josh. 1:1-3)

*Why was Moses called **the servant of the Lord**? Why was Joshua called **Moses' minister**? How did the death of Moses create a leadership crisis for Israel? Why was God's promise to **give** Israel the land conditional on their response? Why is servanthood a characteristic of godly leaders?*

Joshua 1:1-3: Now after the death of Moses the servant of the Lord it came to pass, that the Lord spake unto Joshua the son of Nun, Moses' minister, saying, [2]Moses my servant is dead; now therefore arise, go over this Jordan, thou, and all this people, unto the land which I do give to them, even to the children of Israel. [3]Every place that the sole of your foot shall tread upon, that have I given unto you, as I said unto Moses.

Moses' death was especially traumatic for Israel, for Moses was the only leader they ever had followed. Fortunately, Moses had made careful preparations for the transition to go smoothly. God had led Moses to select Joshua before his death. Moses also made a point of presenting Joshua to the people and stressing that Joshua was his successor. Joshua was well qualified to be the leader at this particular time in the life of Israel. He had had experience in warfare (see Ex. 17:8-14). He had been an assistant to Moses for many years. He and Caleb had proved their faith and courage at Kadesh Barnea.

Just as Moses had the qualities to lead Israel out of Egypt, so did Joshua have the qualities needed as they prepared to cross the Jordan and conquer Canaan. Moses' death is described in Deuteronomy 34:

1-7. Joshua 1:1-3 picks up where Deuteronomy leaves off. God spoke to **Joshua** and said, **Moses my servant is dead; now therefore arise, go over this Jordan, thou, and all this people.** The Jordan River was the eastern border of Canaan and provided a first barrier to be crossed. God used the word **give** to describe what He promised to do with the promised land. However, this giving was conditioned on them trusting and obeying the Lord. Verse 3 is both a promise and a challenge. The promise was that they would receive **every place** on which Joshua's **foot** trod. This was just as God had promised to **Moses.**

The meaning of the words **servant** and **minister** in Hebrew are very similar; however, the title **servant of the LORD** was a more powerful one. This description is used of Moses 17 times in the Book of Joshua. Only at the end of the book is the title used of Joshua (Josh. 24:29). "The relative sociological distance between a 'servant' and his master was far greater than that between an 'aide' and the one he served. Here then is a subtle yet powerful reminder that God's sovereignty is infinite and that he was infinitely greater than even the towering figure of Moses. The gulf between Moses and God was infinitely greater than that between Moses and Joshua."[3] Although Joshua was not Moses, he was able to build on Moses' work to do something that he was better equipped to do than Moses—conquer Canaan.

Each God-called leader is different in some ways, and these differences must not become a basis for dissension in a church. Ideally, each new leader can build on the work of his predecessor and move beyond it to God's will for a new generation.

Moses and Joshua were first of all servants of God, but this made them also servant-leaders of God's people. Jesus repeatedly taught and showed that humble service to others and to God are the marks of true greatness in God's sight (Mark 10:42-45). In Philippians 2:1-11 Paul called on each believer to be a servant to others. Peter warned leaders against lording it over those whom they had been called to lead (1 Pet. 5:3-4). Moses and Joshua are Old Testament examples of servant leaders.

A servant leader points people not to himself but to the Lord. Paul wrote to the Corinthians who were arguing which leader was the best. Paul said one leader sowed the seed and another watered it, but only God makes it grow (1 Cor. 3:1-9). Paul said that he preached Christ, not himself (2 Cor. 4:5). Servant leaders point people to the Lord. Human leaders come and go, but Christ is the same yesterday, today, and forever (Heb. 13:7-8).

Courage (Josh. 1:5-7a,9)

Why is courage an important characteristic of a Christian leader? What is the source of strength to be courageous? What promises did the Lord make to Joshua?

Joshua 1:5-7a,9: There shall not any man be able to stand before thee all the days of thy life: as I was with Moses, so I will be with thee: I will not fail thee, nor forsake thee. ⁶Be strong and of a good courage: for unto this people shalt thou divide for an inheritance the land, which I sware unto their fathers to give them. ⁷Only be thou strong and very courageous. . . . ⁹Have not I commanded thee? Be strong and of a good courage; be not afraid, neither be thou dismayed: for the Lᴏʀᴅ thy God is with thee whithersoever thou goest.

Moses had used these same words in his charge to Joshua (Deut. 31:7-8). Three themes run through these verses. One is the challenge for Joshua to **be strong and of a good courage.** This challenge is found in verses 6,7a, and 9. "The verb 'to be strong' (*hzq*) is common in Hebrew (occurring almost three hundred times), but the verb 'to be courageous' (*'ms*) occurs only forty-one times. Both words are actually similar in meaning."[4]

The second theme is the assurance of the Lord's presence and power in Joshua's life. This promise is made in verse 5: **As I was with Moses, so I will be with thee: I will not fail thee, nor forsake thee.**

The third theme is the victory that will come as a result of the first two themes: **There shall not be any man able to stand before thee** (v. 5), and **for unto this people shalt thou divide for an inheritance the land, which I sware unto their fathers to give them** (v. 6).

Verse 9 repeats the first two themes: **Be strong and of a good courage** is the opposite of fear and discouragement. **Be not afraid, neither be thou dismayed** ("discouraged," NIV): **for the Lᴏʀᴅ thy God is with thee whithersoever thou goest.**

Summing up, the three themes are these: (1) The Lord calls leaders of God's people to be strong and courageous. (2) He promises His presence will be with them. (3) He promises that victory will result from obedience. During Moses' leadership years, he had faced criticism and even rebellion; hopefully the new generation had learned lessons from the fate of their rebellious parents.

Christian leaders must be courageous and strong as they seek to fulfill God's will. Paul often asked believers to pray that he would be able to bear bold testimony for the Lord. The presence and power of the Lord are necessary to fulfill God's purpose. Victory comes when leaders act with courage that comes from the Lord. Those who follow leaders must be willing to follow bold leadership for the Lord.

Obedience to Scriptures (Josh. 1:7b-8)

What was the law? What was Joshua to do with the law? What kind of success did God promise him?

Joshua 1:7b-8: **That thou mayest observe to do according to all the law, which Moses my servant commanded thee: turn not from it to the right hand or to the left, that thou mayest prosper whithersoever thou goest. ⁸This book of the law shall not depart out of thy mouth; but thou shalt meditate therein day and night, that thou mayest observe to do according to all that is written therein: for then thou shalt make thy way prosperous, and then thou shalt have good success.**

The basic message of these verses is **observe to do according to all the law. The law** here refers to the commands God gave to Israel when He made the covenant with them. In verse 8, **this book of the law** is mentioned. This may refer to the books of the Pentateuch or to part of them. Joshua was with Moses when he came down from the mountain with the Ten Commandments. As assistant to Moses, he knew what God expected of His people. For us **the law** represents the Scriptures, which means the Old and New Testaments.

Joshua was commanded **not** to **turn** either **to the right hand or to the left.** In other words, he was to move straight ahead in obeying the law. He was not to deviate from that course. God's law should **not depart out of** his **mouth.** He should live it and share it with others. He was to **meditate therein day and night.**

Verse 8 repeats two things from verse 7. One is the importance of obeying the law. The other is a promise of success and prosperity if he did these things. By obeying the law, Joshua was promised that he would **prosper** wherever he went (v. 7). Verse 8 reiterates, **Thou shalt make thy way prosperous, and then thou shalt have good success. Prosperity** and **success** are words that catch the ear of people today. People aspire to be prosperous and successful. Thus we need to be careful about applying these words today. Some people have interpreted this promise as material prosperity and worldly success;

however, "the two words we find here in our passage in Joshua (1:7-8) speaking of prosperity and success are almost never used in the Old Testament to speak of financial success. Rather, they speak of succeeding in life's proper endeavors. This happens when people's lives are focused entirely on God and obedience to him."[5]

The point of these verses in this lesson is that godly leaders know and do what God says in His Word. They **meditate on** God's Word **day and night.** They live by it and teach others to do so. Living a Christian life is not easy in a sinful world. Leaders must set the right examples. To do that, they must live in the Word of God. All Christians should do the same. In this way, the people follow God as He reveals Himself in His Word.

Trustworthiness (Josh. 1:16-17)

What group did the speaking in these verses? Why might they be tempted not to follow through with their commitments? What promises did they make to Joshua? How do their words show that they considered Joshua as a trustworthy leader?

Joshua 1:16-17: And they answered Joshua, saying, All that thou commandest us we will do, and whithersoever thou sendest us, we will go. [17]According as we hearkened unto Moses in all things, so will we hearken unto thee: only the Lord thy God be with thee, as he was with Moses.

The context shows that the speakers in verses 16-17 were those Israelites who had chosen to settle on the east side of the Jordan River (see vv. 12-15). The tribes of Reuben, Gad, and half of the tribe of Manasseh had made a special request of Moses. They asked to be allowed to settle on the east side of the Jordan. Moses spoke plainly to them. He allowed them to settle their families there on one condition—that the fighting men of these tribes cross the river and help the other tribes conquer Canaan. They promised to do this (Num. 32). Now that Moses was dead, these Israelites repeated their promise to the new leader, Joshua. They promised to **do** whatever Joshua commanded and to **go** wherever he sent them. They showed their trust in Joshua by saying they would obey Joshua just as they had Moses. Their prayer and trust was that **the Lord** would **be with** Joshua as He had been **with Moses.**

An effective leader must have the trust of those who follow him. Without trust people cease to hear and heed what the leader says. When a new leader comes into a situation in which the past leader had proven trustworthy, it is easier for the people to trust the new leader. This was the situation with Joshua, who was privileged to succeed Moses and who had won the respect and trust of the people. On the other hand, if a new leader follows a previous leader who broke trust with the people, earning their trust is more difficult.

Being trustworthy is essential for people to follow their leader. We should not expect a new leader to be like his predecessor. If an earlier leader proved untrustworthy, don't be prejudiced and suspicious of his successor. If an earlier leader was a good and effective leader, do not expect the new leader to be just like his predecessor. Give a new leader the benefit of the doubt by trusting that he will prove trustworthy.

❖ Spiritual Transformations

Before Moses died, the Lord led him to publicly name Joshua as his successor. Both Moses and Joshua were servants of God and of others. God challenged Joshua to be strong and courageous because the Lord was with him. God commanded Joshua to meditate on and obey His law. The people transferred their trust from Moses to Joshua.

Here are some of the teachings about following godly leaders:
• When a new leader is needed, pray that the Lord will reveal him.
• When a new leader is called, present him as the one whom God called.
• A godly leader is a servant-leader who serves God and people.
• The courage and strength of a godly leader come from God's presence and power.
• A godly leader lives by the Word of God.
• A godly leader is trustworthy and should be trusted.

What do you consider the most important qualities of godly leaders?
_____

How can you do better in supporting and following godly leaders in your church? _____

Prayer of Commitment: Lord, help me to be a godly person and to follow godly leaders.

[1]Ashley, *The Book of Numbers*, 553.
[2]Roy B. Zuck, *The Speaker's Quote Book* [Grand Rapids: Kregel Publications, 1997], 226.
[3]David M. Howard, Jr., "Joshua," in the *New American Commentary*, vol. 5 [Nashville: Broadman & Holman Publishers, 1998], 75.
[4]Howard, "Joshua," NAC, 84.
[5]Howard, "Joshua," NAC, 88.

Leaving a Legacy

Background Passage: Joshua 3:1–4:24
Focal Passage: Joshua 3:9-10a,14-17; 4:15-24
Key Verse: Joshua 4:24

❖ *Significance of the Lesson*

• The *Theme* of this lesson is that people who obey God demonstrate His power and thereby influence future generations through their obedience.

• The *Life Question* this lesson seeks to address is, To whom does my obedience to God matter?

• The *Biblical Truth* is that obedience to God influences one's contemporaries and provides a legacy of faithfulness to succeeding generations.

• The *Life Impact* is to help you leave a legacy of obedience to God.

Leaving a Legacy

The dictionary gives two basic definitions of the word *legacy*. One is a gift by will, especially of money or other personal property. The other is something received from an ancestor or predecessors or from the past.

In a secular worldview, people often are concerned to leave a legacy of material things. They have less concern about leaving a legacy of moral and spiritual values.

In a biblical worldview, believers want to leave for their children and future generations a legacy of faith and obedience to God. They thus take actions to leave this kind of legacy.

Word Study: *The Living God*

Calling God *the living God,* as in Joshua 3:10, emphasizes that He is not dead and nonexistent like the false gods of pagans. Images of false gods are made by humans from wood and stone. They are lifeless and unable to hear or to help those who worship them.

❖ Search the Scriptures

The Israelites trusted and obeyed God by entering the Jordan River at flood stage and passing safely through as the Lord stopped the river's flow. Joshua commanded that 12 stones be set up as a memorial to teach future generations what the Lord had done. Word of this miracle would be a testimony to all nations of the Lord's power.

Acting in Obedience (Josh. 3:9-10a,14-17)

*What is the significance of the title **the living God**? What led the people as they went into the Jordan River? What is the significance of the river being at flood stage? When did the waters of the river stop?*

3:9-10a: And Joshua said unto the children of Israel, Come hither, and hear the words of the LORD your God. ¹⁰And Joshua said, Hereby ye shall know that the living God is among you.

The long years of wandering were over. At last the Israelites stood poised to enter the promised land. Yet ahead of them were two barriers—the Jordan River at flood stage and the fortified city of Jericho.

Joshua sent officers throughout the camp to instruct the people about the procedure for crossing the river. Taking the lead would be the ark of the covenant carried by the priests. "Two thousand cubits" ("a thousand yards," NIV) behind came the people (v. 4). Meanwhile, Joshua ordered the people to sanctify themselves. God promised that when the feet of the priests carrying the ark went into the river that He would cause the waters to stand up and that one result of this would be that the people would know for sure that Joshua was God's chosen leader for them as they entered the promised land (3:1-8).

Joshua said unto the children of Israel, Come hither, and hear the words of the LORD your God. The Hebrew word for **hear** means more than just receiving a message with one's ears. When used of hearing God, it means not only to *hear* but also to *obey* the word of the Lord.

Joshua spoke with the authority of God, whom he called **the living God.** "There is no article in Hebrew in the phrase 'the living God' (v. 10). Without the article emphasis is placed on the fact that Israel's God is *living*. Joshua is not simply stating that the living God is *with* them. He is affirming that the God who marches with Israel is one who is able to act and to perform mighty deeds in contrast to the pagan gods that have eyes but cannot see."[1]

The results of their obedience would be that they would **know that the living God** was **among** them. This would be the first result of their obedience. Later the Word of the Lord showed that this miracle would also make God known to people other than the Israelites and also to the descendants of the Israelites in future generations.

3:14-17: **And it came to pass, when the people removed from their tents, to pass over Jordan, and the priests bearing the ark of the covenant before the people;** [15]**and as they that bare the ark were come unto Jordan, and the feet of the priests that bare the ark were dipped in the brim of the water, (for Jordan overfloweth all his banks all the time of harvest,)** [16]**that the waters which came down from above stood and rose up upon an heap very far from the city Adam, that is beside Zaretan: and those that came down toward the sea of the plain, even the salt sea, failed, and were cut off: and the people passed over right against Jericho.** [17]**And the priests that bare the ark of the covenant of the LORD stood firm on dry ground in the midst of Jordan, and all the Israelites passed over on dry ground, until all the people were passed clean over Jordan.**

Verse 14 shows that the priests and people followed instructions about the line of march. **The people** came out of **their tents** and they followed **the priests bearing the ark of the covenant.** Notice when the waters stopped flowing. This did not happen until **the feet of the priests that bare the ark were dipped in the brim of the water.** "Now the Jordan is at flood stage all during harvest. Yet as soon as the priests who carried the ark reached the Jordan and their feet touched the water's edge, the water from upstream stopped flowing" (NIV). Marching forward into a river at flood stage required faith and obedience. The waters did not part and then the priests moved forward. The waters parted only when their feet touched the swift waters of the river at flood stage. The Jordan River at this point had only a few places to ford even when the river was at its normal depth. However, now the river was out of its banks and impossible to ford in the normal way.

The manner of the miracle is described in verse 16: **The waters which came down from above stood and rose up upon an heap** ("The waters which came down from upstream stood still, and rose in a heap," NKJV; "The water from upstream stopped flowing. It piled up in a heap," NIV). John J. Davis mentioned three ways of looking at the biblical account. "There are those who deny the whole event as being purely fictitious. Others assert that God used a natural phenomenon; that is, an earthquake actually caused the crumbling of some of the cliffs in the northern part of the Jordan thereby blocking the waters and permitting Israel to cross. . . . On July 11, 1927, a landslide near the ford at Damiyeh was caused by an earthquake, and the flow was blocked for twenty-one hours. While such an event is possible, one must agree that the timing would have to be a miracle. . . . The third view is that the event should be regarded as basically supernatural in nature, that is; the Lord, by causes unknown to us, stopped the flow of the Jordan for a sufficient amount of time to enable the Israelites to cross safely."[2]

Verse 16 tells us that **the waters . . . rose up upon an heap very far from the city Adam. Very far from** probably refers to distance from where the crossing took place. The *New King James Version* has "very far away at Adam." This cut off the flow of the river **toward the sea of the plain.** This **sea** is also known as **the salt sea** or what we call the Dead Sea. The place where the Israelites were was **right against** ("opposite," NIV, NKJV) **Jericho.**

Another evidence of the miracle was that the river bed was not muddy but dry. When the priests carrying the ark reached the middle of the river bed, they **stood firm on dry ground.** Further, **all the Israelites passed over on dry ground.**

The important thing to note about these verses is the faith and obedience of the people, which allowed the Lord to work this miracle. God gives us many good things apart from our faith, but His best gifts are conditioned on our faith and obedience. Faith that does not obey the Lord is not true faith. If the priests had not walked into the swollen river, would God have stopped the water? We cannot know, but we do know that He stopped the flow only when they moved forward in faith.

Influencing Descendants (Josh. 4:15-22)

When did the waters begin to flow again? What special task did Joshua assign to 12 men? What is the significance of the date when they crossed the river? What was done with the stones from the Jordan? How does this passage emphasize sharing a legacy of faith and obedience?

4:15-22: And the LORD spake unto Joshua, saying, ¹⁶Command the priests that bear the ark of the testimony, that they come up out of Jordan. ¹⁷Joshua therefore commanded the priests, saying, Come ye up out of Jordan. ¹⁸And it came to pass, when the priests

that bare the ark of the covenant of the Lᴏʀᴅ were come up out of the midst of Jordan, and the soles of the priests' feet were lifted up unto the dry land, that the waters of Jordan returned unto their place, and flowed over all his banks, as they did before. [19]And the people came up out of Jordan on the tenth day of the first month, and encamped in Gilgal, in the east border of Jericho. [20]And those twelve stones, which they took out of Jordan, did Joshua pitch in Gilgal. [21]And he spake unto the children of Israel, saying, When your children shall ask their fathers in time to come, saying, What mean these stones? [22]Then ye shall let your children know, saying, Israel came over this Jordan on dry land.

Joshua 4:1-14 tells several facts that help understand the Focal Passage. The Lord commanded Joshua to enlist 12 men—one from each tribe—to carry 12 stones from the river bed (vv. 1-8). Included among the Israelites were the fighting men of Reuben, Gad, and half of the tribe of Manasseh. They were doing what they had promised Moses and Joshua—entering Canaan to help conquer the land as a whole. Their families had settled on the eastern bank of the Jordan. Joshua also had 12 stones set up in the midst of the Jordan River where the feet of the priests who carried the ark of the covenant had stood (v. 9). One result of this successful entry into Canaan was that the Lord magnified Joshua and confirmed that he was God's chosen leader for the conquest of Canaan (v. 14).

The priests and the ark stayed in the midst of the river bed until all the Israelites had passed safely over into Canaan. Then the Lord commanded Joshua to call the priests to **come . . . up out of Jordan.** The priests obeyed. Just standing in the middle of the river bed must have taken courage and faith. Yet they had been faithful, and God held back the waters until the priests came out of the river bed. However, just as the waters stopped when their feet touched the water, the waters began to flow again as soon as **the soles of the priests' feet were lifted up unto the dry land.** The water then **flowed over all his banks, as they did before.** This was another evidence of the hand of God.

The crossing of the Jordan took place **on the tenth day of the first month.** That was the date for the selection of a lamb for celebrating Passover. They celebrated this important feast a few days later (Josh. 5:10-12). This served to tie the crossing of the Jordan River to the earlier miracle of the crossing of the Red Sea. The relation of the two miracles is spelled out in 4:23.

The people camped at **Gilgal.** There they set up the **twelve stones which they took out of Jordan.** These stones formed a kind of memorial of the crossing of the Jordan River. Their purpose was not only to remind the people who had taken part in the crossing but also to be a means of teaching future generations what the Lord had done. Future generations would see these 12 stones and **ask their fathers . . . What mean these stones?** This question provided an opportunity for telling future generations how **Israel came over this Jordan on dry land.**

These stones would be the means of sharing their legacy of faith and obedience with their children and with future generations of children. Thus it had a purpose like that of the Passover meal, which reminded the Israelites of their deliverance from Egypt. One purpose of the Passover was to lead children to ask questions that provided an opportunity to teach the children about what God had done (Ex. 13:14).

The application of this stone memorial, therefore, was to leave a legacy of faith and obedience. Both the Old Testament and the New Testament emphasize the responsibility of parents to leave such a legacy for their children, grandchildren, and future generations.

All parents leave some kind of legacy for their children. It may be a legacy of sin and unbelief, or it may be a legacy of faith and godliness. Deuteronomy 6:5-9 commanded Israelite parents to speak of their faith to their children. Joshua himself was an example of a father who was committed to God and led his household to share his commitment (Josh. 24:15). In the New Testament, fathers were told to bring their children up in the nurture and admonition of the Lord (Eph. 6:4). Timothy's faith was a legacy from his mother and grandmother (2 Tim. 1:5).

Parenting is a great responsibility. Responsible parents want to leave a worthy legacy for their children. Many think only of the money and property left in their estate. But a moral and spiritual legacy is more important. James Dobson is right in what he said about many parents who were raised in Christian homes but who neglect to give the same legacy to their children because they are too busy working to buy themselves and their children a high standard of living: "We are so busy giving our children what we never had that we forget to give them what we did have."[3]

One of the tragedies of life is when parents fail to give to their children what God wants every child to have. Parents owe their children to love God, each other, and their children. This takes an investment of time and energy, a life of faith and love, and teaching the children by word and deed.

When I was a young pastor, I heard some older pastors talking about the terrible behavior of people when a loved one dies. They said that family members are often at their worst as they greedily seek as much of the estate as they can get for themselves. Jesus met a man who asked Him to tell his brother to give him his portion of his inheritance. Jesus warned the man against covetousness (Luke 12:13-15).

Many people have not made a will. This is unwise because without a will, the state will divide one's estate in ways the deceased did not intend. But even more important than a will dealing with money and property is a legacy of faith and obedience to God. This cannot be left in a written document.

Catherine Marshall told of her experience of going through her father's things after his death. She mentioned two things that impressed her. One was his checkbook, showing a balance of 65 cents. Her father was a minister who never had much of the world's goods. She also found a letter she had written to him not long before his death. She was glad that she had written this while he still could read it. In her letter she had written these words: "You and Mother gave me the most gorgeous childhood any little girl ever had, because you gave so much of yourself. . . . But of course, the greatest thing that you and Mother did for us was to bequeath us the sure knowledge of the love and goodness of God abroad in the world."[4]

Last year my parents celebrated their 70th wedding anniversary. They received many cards and letters from family and friends. One of our grown children wrote them a letter that especially impressed them. When I read what Thomas had written to his grandparents, I too thanked God. In the letter Thomas mentioned a song written by an entertainer on the family tradition begun by his father. It was anything but Christian. Then Thomas spoke of the family tradition in which he had been raised. He wrote: "I can see a tradition of faith in God and love for family being passed down like an inheritance to my siblings, my cousins, and to me. It is a blessing beyond all possible earthly value."

Robbie Trent's book on *Your Child and God* was written over half a century ago, but most of what she wrote is timeless. For example, she wrote this list of things that a child needs to become committed to Jesus Christ:
- Christian example of parents
- Pleasant and open relationship with parents
- Home religious training suited to his age

- Parents who share what religion means to them
- Regular church attendance
- Hearing Bible read in the home
- Group prayer in the home
- Blessing at the table
- Hearing Bible stories in the home
- Religious conversation in the home
- A home which reflects God's standards
- Parents who enjoy their religion
- Personal prayer experiences
- Sympathetic and honest meeting of questions in the home.[5]

Testifying to the World (Josh. 4:23-24)

*How was crossing the Jordan compared to the crossing of the Red Sea? What message did God intend that these two miracles communicate to **people of the earth**?*

4:23-24: For the LORD your God dried up the waters of Jordan from before you, until ye were passed over, as the LORD your God did to the Red sea, which he dried up from before us, until we were gone over: [24]that all the people of the earth might know the hand of the LORD, that it is mighty: that ye might fear the LORD your God forever.

Verse 23 spells out the likeness of the miracles of Israel's crossing the **Jordan** and the **Red sea.** Some of the people who crossed over the Jordan into the promised land remembered crossing the Red Sea. Joshua and Caleb surely did. And since those who were under 20 years of age survived the judgment of death in the wilderness, some of them were old enough when they left Egypt to remember what happened. Many of this group were not with the group who left Egypt; however, the Passover was designed to teach them what the Lord had done in delivering their parents from Egyptian bondage. This included the miracles of the plagues (especially the death of the firstborn) and the parting of the Red Sea. Both the crossing of the Jordan River and the crossing of the Red Sea involved miracles of the Lord on behalf of His people. Both events were to be remembered and taught to each new generation.

Both events also were testimonies **that all the people of the earth might know the hand of the LORD, that it is mighty.** Of course these events also were directed to Israel: **that ye might fear the LORD thy God forever.** The interesting thing in verse 24 is the mentioning of the intended purpose of God for people other than the Israelites. God wanted non-Israelites to hear of these mighty acts of God on behalf of His people and become aware of God and His power. This verse alone is not a clear call for missionary work, but it is a biblical testimony to God's purpose to include all people. Scattered throughout the Old Testament are clear signs that the God of Israel intended to be the God of all people. In the New Testament, the Great Commission clearly commands believers to take the good news of God to all nations.

❖ *Spiritual Transformations*

When the Israelites acted in faith and obedience by marching into the flooded Jordan River, the Lord stopped the river's flow until all could pass safely over. As God had instructed, they built a memorial of 12 stones as a way of leaving a legacy of faith and obedience to future generations. The purpose of the crossing of the Jordan was that the Israelites might fear the Lord and that people of other nations would hear about the power of the God of Israel.

The Life Impact of this lesson is that you and I leave a legacy of faith and obedience to God. We owe this to our own children and grandchildren and to others in future generations.

In what ways have you sought to leave such a legacy? _____

Look at the list made by Robbie Trent on pages 33-34. Put a check mark by the ones that you have done or are doing.

In what ways do you intend to do more than you have done? ____
_____

*What questions have children asked you? How well did you use these opportunities?*_____

Prayer of Commitment: Lord, I am grateful for those who taught me about You. Help me to do my part in sharing You with my children, grandchildren, and others of younger generations.

[1]Donald H. Madvig, "Joshua," in *The Expositor's Bible Commentary*, vol. 3 [Grand Rapids: Zondervan Publishing House, 1992], 266.

[2]John J. Davis, *Conquest and Crisis: Studies in Joshua, Judges, and Ruth* [Grand Rapids: Baker Book House, 1969], 38.

[3]Zuck, *The Speaker's Quote Book*, 279.

[4]Catherine Marshall, *Beyond Our Selves* [New York: McGraw-Hill Book Company, Inc., 1961], 254-255.

[5]Robbie Trent, *Your Child and God* [New York: Harper & Brothers Publishers, 1952], 156.

Obeying Totally

Background Passage: Joshua 6:1-27
Focal Passage: Joshua 6:1-5,14-21,24-25
Key Verse: Joshua 6:2

❖ *Significance of the Lesson*

• The *Theme* of this lesson is that we are to obey all that God commands, even if we don't understand all the reasons for His commands.
• The *Life Question* this lesson seeks to address is, To what extent should I obey God?
• The *Biblical Truth* is that God expects His people always to obey all His commands, even if they don't understand all the reasons for His commands.
• *The Life Impact* is to help you obey God completely, even if you don't understand all the reasons for His commands.

Unquestioning Obedience to God

In a secular worldview, obeying God is not a consideration at all. People with a secular worldview try to avoid being confronted with God's commands; and when they are confronted, they find excuses to ignore God's will. Even many believers try to pick and choose which commands they will obey.

According to the biblical worldview, true believers seek to hear God's commands in order to obey God. His commands are in the Bible, and God expects His people to obey His Word. Believers do not always understand the reasons for the commands, but true believers trust and obey even though they may not know the reasons.

Word Study: *Haram / Herem*

In Joshua 6:17,18, and 21, the words "accursed," "accursed thing," "curse," and "utterly destroyed" translate the important Hebrew verb *haram* or the noun *herem.* "The verb can be rendered 'to devote to the LORD' or 'to devote to destruction' or 'to completely destroy,' and the noun can be rendered as 'devoted things' or 'destruction.' The NIV text note makes clear the connection between the idea of devotion and destruction: 'The Hebrew term refers to the irrevocable giving over of things or persons to the LORD, often by totally destroying them.'"[1] According to David M. Howard, Jr., "The NRSV's rendering in v. 17a captures the nuances: 'And the city, and all that is within it shall be devoted to the LORD for destruction.'"[2]

The Command to Destroy All People and Things

How can we explain this extreme command to Joshua and the Israelites? It seems contradictory to the revelation of a loving God in the New Testament. David M. Howard, Jr., writing in the *New American Commentary,* offered insight into this difficult question. For one thing, he pointed out that the sins of the Canaanites had reached such a low level that they deserved severe punishment. Closely related was the fact that if the Canaanites remained in the land, their sins would provide a constant temptation for the Israelites to compromise their own distinctive way of life. A third factor was that the Lord had given the city of Jericho into the hands of the Israelites, and the Israelites could signify that by devoting all the people and wealth of Jericho to God.

Several additional factors help to take some of the edge off the command. For one thing, not everyone in Jericho was among those to be put to death. Specific commands were given to spare the life of Rahab and her family because she hid the Hebrew spies and because she professed faith in the God of Israel. Her salvation testifies to God's intention eventually to open the door of faith to all people. Further, not every Israelite was spared. Achan and his family were put to death because they disobeyed God. Another qualifying factor is that this command applied to one stage of the history of Israel. The full revelation of God in Jesus Christ calls for loving testimony to all people.[3]

❖ *Search the Scriptures*

God told Joshua and the Israelites what to do to conquer Jericho. They carefully obeyed Him. God warned against disobedience. The wall fell and the city was taken.

Obey in Seemingly Hopeless Situations (Josh. 6:1-5)

What was the larger setting and immediate context for this passage? Why was Jericho such a formidable barrier to Israel's plans to conquer Canaan? In what sense had God already given the Israelites the city of Jericho? How did God's commands about taking the city differ from usual military ways of capturing a walled city?

Verse 1: Now Jericho was straitly shut up because of the children of Israel: none went out, and none came in.

Before entering Canaan, Joshua had sent two spies to Jericho. A prostitute named Rahab, who had faith in the Lord, hid them. They promised to spare her and her family when the city was taken.

After crossing the Jordan, the Israelites spent several days in Gilgal. During that time they set themselves apart for the Lord by circumcision (5:2-9). They also celebrated the Passover (vv. 10-11). The manna ceased on the day they were able to eat the food in Canaan (v. 12).

Jericho was located strategically to guard the eastern entrance to Canaan. The Israelites could not afford to bypass this city, for to do so would leave a powerful enemy force in their rear. Jericho was a walled city that was fortified to withstand invaders. The city was **straitly** ("tightly," NIV) **shut up** ("shut up inside and out," NRSV; "bolted and barred," NEB). This means that the gates were closed and made strong. That **none went out, and none came in** shows that the Israelites were kept outside the city and the people of the city were kept inside.

This city was soon to be under siege. They responded as would a city expecting to be surrounded by a powerful enemy. Often a besieged city allowed foraging parties to venture forth to get food or a raiding party to harass the enemy. Thus the tightly closed city revealed something about the people of Jericho and something about the challenge to the Israelites. It revealed that the people of Jericho had heard of the victories of the Israelites and were taking no chances. Rahab told the two spies when they had visited her earlier that the people melted in fear of the Israelites (2:9). The people of Jericho also had heard of the Israelites' miraculous crossing of the Jordan River and this made them even more fearful (5:1). God used this fear to deliver the city to His people.

Verses 2-5: And the LORD said unto Joshua, See, I have given into thine hand Jericho, and the king thereof, and the mighty men of valor. ³And ye shall compass the city, all ye men of war, and go round about the city once. Thus shalt thou do six days. ⁴And seven

priests shall bear before the ark seven trumpets of rams' horns: and the seventh day ye shall compass the city seven times, and the priests shall blow with the trumpets. [5]And it shall come to pass, that when they make a long blast with the ram's horn, and when ye hear the sound of the trumpet, all the people shall shout with a great shout; and the wall of the city shall fall down flat, and the people shall ascend up every man straight before him.

The LORD said unto Joshua shows that verses 2-5 were addressed to Joshua. Later he passed these commands and promises along to the people. I have given is stronger than saying "I will give." The fall of the city was yet to take place, but it was so sure that the Lord could speak of it as already done. Included among those whom the Lord gave to His people were the king thereof, and the mighty men of valor. Thus God promised not only to bring down the wall but also to destroy the fighting men of the city.

Verses 3-5 are the instructions that God gave for taking the city. Compass was to "march around" (NIV, NKJV). Israel's men of war were to march around the city once a day for each of six days. Seven priests were to have seven trumpets of rams' horns. These seven trumpeters were to go ahead of the ark. This was the ark of the covenant, which signified the presence of the Lord. It played an important role at Jericho just as it had in crossing the Jordan. On the seventh day they were to go around the city seven times. Then the priests were to blow with the trumpets.

Seven is a repeated number in this biblical passage. This number is used often in the Bible, and seems to have represented perfection and completeness. Marten H. Woudstra saw a connection to Genesis and God's work of creation: "The number seven is doubtless symbolical, recalling God's works at creation. The Lord who creates also works in the history of redemption. On the seventh day he will act on his people's behalf."[4]

The priests were then to make a long blast with the ram's horn. This would be the signal for the people to shout with a great shout. When this was done as God had commanded, God promised Joshua that the wall of the city shall fall down flat, and the people shall ascend up every man straight before him ("every man straight in," NIV).

The Israelites were facing their first foes in the land of Canaan. Their enemies were safely within a walled city, which seemed to be impossible to conquer. Yet the Lord commanded Joshua to tell them what to do for the Lord to give them victory.

Joshua and the people were commanded to do some strange things. They had to trust God's word and to move ahead with obedience. On what could they base their trust and obedience? They could remember how the Lord already had done some impossible things for them. He had delivered the enslaved Israelites from Egypt, the most powerful nation on earth. The exodus was always spoken of as a divine deliverance, not a human victory or escape. He had led them through the Red Sea and more recently through the Jordan River at flood stage. The memory of these deliverances encouraged them to dare to trust and obey God to use these unusual actions to give them Jericho.

Persist in Obedience (Josh. 6:14-16)

How did Joshua pass along to the people the commands of the Lord for taking Jericho? Why is there so much repetition in the biblical account? How were besieged cities usually taken by military means? What do these verses reveal about the response of the Israelites to God's commands?

Verses 14-16: And the second day they compassed the city once, and returned into the camp: so they did six days. ¹⁵And it came to pass on the seventh day, that they rose early about the dawning of the day, and compassed the city after the same manner seven times: only on that day they compassed the city seven times. ¹⁶And it came to pass at the seventh time, when the priests blew with the trumpets, Joshua said unto the people, Shout; for the LORD hath given you the city.

Verses 6-7 summarize Joshua's words to the priests and to the people. Verses 8-9 describe the obedience of priests and people. The order of march was fighting men, seven priests with trumpets, the ark, and a rear guard. The people were told to remain quiet until the seventh day, when they were to shout loudly (v. 10). These verses describe the first day. Verses 12-13 describe what the people did each day.

Verse 14 summarizes their actions on **the second day.** As God had commanded, they marched around **the city once, and returned into the camp. So they did six days,** exactly as the Lord had commanded.

They got an **early** start on **the seventh day.** Whereas on days one through six they marched only once around Jericho, **on that day they compassed the city seven times.** On each day prior to the seventh day, the same thing had been done. They marched around the city once with the people silent but with the trumpets blaring. On the seventh day they went around seven times; then all seven trumpeters sounded a long blast. The people, who had been silent for six days, were told, **Shout; for the LORD hath given you the city.**

If you had been Joshua or one of the people, what would you have been tempted to ask about these instructions for taking Jericho? Can you imagine what questions and objections would have been spoken by the generation who had refused to enter Canaan at Kadesh Barnea? Yet there is no record of any Israelite asking questions or raising objections about this most unusual strategy for taking a walled city.

We have no record of what the people of Jericho said and felt on the six days or on the seventh. Nor are we told how the Israelites felt. Both groups knew that the Israelites were not acting like a besieging army usually acted during a siege. Several military strategies were used to break into a walled city. The invaders often tried to breach the wall at some point and then to pour troops through that break in the wall. Sometimes besiegers tried to use ladders to scale the walls or tunnels to go under the walls. When these failed, invaders sometimes tried to starve out the people inside the walls. At times, spies or traitors opened the gates or some other way for the invaders to enter.

If you had been a citizen of Jericho, what would you have felt about what the Israelites were doing? If you were an Israelite, what would you have felt about obeying Joshua's unusual commands? Whatever they felt, they obeyed, even though they did not understand the reasons for doing so—and what is more, they persisted in obeying the Lord's commands day after day.

Samuel Johnson wisely said, "Nothing will ever be attempted if all possible objections must first be overcome."[5]

Heed Warnings Against Disobedience (Josh. 6:17-19)

*In what sense was the city of Jericho **accursed**? In light of later biblical revelation, how can we justify such drastic actions as were taken at Jericho? What is the significance of saving **Rahab**? What warning was given to the Israelites? How was this broken by one man? What was to be done with the gold and silver?*

Verse 17: And the city shall be accursed, even it, and all that are therein, to the LORD: only Rahab the harlot shall live, she and all that are with her in the house, because she hid the messengers that we sent.

The word **accursed** is explained in the Word Study. The Hebrew word referred to dedicating everyone and everything in Jericho to the Lord. In the case of people, and most possessions, this meant that all were to be destroyed. The sins of the people of Canaan were so abhorrent that they deserved death. Their sins were evil as far back as the time of Abraham, but the Lord told Abraham that their sins were not yet complete (Gen. 15:16). However, by the time of Joshua, they were complete. Leviticus 18:3-23 lists some of their sins: incest, adultery, child sacrifice, homosexual behavior, and bestiality. The Israelites were commanded to abstain from these sins (Lev. 18:24-30). God knew that if the Canaanites were allowed to remain in the land, their evil would be a constant temptation to the Israelites. Therefore, God told Israel to destroy all these peoples (Deut. 7:1-5; 20:16-20). The Israelites failed to destroy all of them, and they became a source of the temptation and sin that eventually caused the Lord to send judgment on His own people (Judg. 2:2-3).

Israel was called to be God's special people who could bear witness to the nations for the Lord and of His ways. Before the exile, Israel continually failed to be such a people. They kept compromising their faith and way of life. Thus they were not able to become a missionary nation. Stern measures against the evil Canaanites, and later against the sinful Israelites, were necessary to lead to a time when salvation was offered to all people.

The last part of verse 17 shows that the destruction of the people of Jericho did not include **Rahab** and her family. Her story is in Joshua 2. She hid the two Israelite spies whom Joshua had sent to Jericho. Rahab was a Gentile and a prostitute, but she and her family were the only people in Jericho who were saved. She bore witness to the spies not only of her own faith but also of the terror that the people of Jericho felt.

Rahab's salvation is a sign of hope that God's purpose eventually would include believers from all people. It is thus a light shining in the darkness of the destruction of the pagan people of Jericho.

Verses 18-19: And ye, in any wise keep yourselves from the accursed thing, lest ye make yourselves accursed, when ye take of the accursed thing, and make the camp of Israel a curse, and trouble it. ¹⁹But all the silver, and gold, and vessels of brass and iron, are consecrated unto the LORD: they shall come into the treasury of the LORD.

Verse 18 was a warning to the Israelites. They had been commanded by God to destroy everyone and everything in Jericho. They were warned against disobeying that command. To do so would bring a curse on the guilty one and on Israel as a whole. David Howard offered this translation of verse 18 showing the key Hebrew word in this lesson's Word Study: "But keep away from *the devoted things [herem]*, so that you will not *bring about your own destruction [haram]* by taking any of *[the devoted things (herem)]*. Otherwise you will make the camp of Israel liable to *destruction [herem]* and bring trouble on it."[6]

Joshua 7 tells the tragic story of one Israelite who disobeyed God's command. Achan could not resist taking some silver, gold, and clothes for himself. His sin—unknown to Joshua at the time—led to Israel's defeat at Ai. When Achan's sin was revealed, he and all his family were put to death. This shows that disobedience—whether by Canaanites or Israelites—was deadly.

The only exceptions to the command to destroy all things were **all the silver, and gold, and vessels of brass and iron.** These were **consecrated unto the LORD.** They eventually came **into the treasury of the LORD.**

Just as faith and obedience led to glory for the Lord and blessings for the people, so did disobedience lead to death. Achan probably thought that no one would ever find out about his sin, but the Lord knew. Oh how God's people need to heed His warnings against disobedience to His commands!

Reap Victory Through Obedience (Josh. 6:20-21,24-25)

Who or what brought down the wall of Jericho? How was the city taken? How complete was the destruction? Why is so much attention given to Rahab? What is the significance of her salvation?

Verses 20-21: So the people shouted when the priests blew with the trumpets: and it came to pass, when the people heard the sound of the trumpet, and the people shouted with a great shout, that the wall fell down flat, so that the people went up into the city, every man straight before him, and they took the city. ²¹And they utterly destroyed all that was in the city, both man and woman, young and old, and ox, and sheep, and ass, with the edge of the sword.

Verse 20 picks up the action from verse 16. The Israelites followed the commands of God to the letter. They had marched around the city in the order of march set forth by God. The trumpeters had sounded on each day, and the people were silent. Then on the seventh day they went around seven times. Then a loud blast on the trumpets was followed by **a great shout** by the people. Then **the wall fell down flat, so that the people went up into the city, every man straight before him.** Since the Israelites were all around the city, each of the armed men attacked at the point of his place when the wall fell down. **They took the city,** just as the Lord had promised. The men of Jericho were frightened by the Israelites even before they came. Their fear must have grown with each day of the march around the city. Then when the people marched around seven times, they feared the worst, which is just what happened. The context implies they did not put up much of a fight after the wall fell.

The Israelites followed the directions they had been given (with the exception of Achan). They destroyed all the people (except Rahab and her family) and all the livestock.

Verses 24-25: **And they burnt the city with fire, and all that was therein: only the silver, and the gold, and the vessels of brass and of iron, they put into the treasury of the house of the LORD. [25]And Joshua saved Rahab the harlot alive, and her father's household, and all that she had; and she dwelleth in Israel even unto this day; because she hid the messengers, which Joshua sent to spy out Jericho.**

The victorious Israelites **burnt the city with fire,** after they had taken out all the valuables to be placed **into the treasury of the house of the LORD.**

Verse 25 returns to **Rahab.** The amount of space given to the story of Rahab shows her importance. Richard S. Hess noted: "Eighty-six words in the Hebrew text are devoted to Rahab's rescue, while the destruction of Jericho occupies 102. The account concludes with Rahab. The salvation of Rahab was as important as the destruction of Jericho."[7]

Rahab's long-range importance is seen by her inclusion in the genealogy of Jesus in Matthew 1:1-17. She is one of three women, other than Mary, who are referred to. Thamar (v. 3; "Tamar," NIV), Ruth (v. 5), and the wife of Urias (v. 6; "Uriah's wife," NIV) are the others. This inclusion of women in Jesus' genealogy signifies His mission to save sinners from all nations. Rahab was not only a Canaanite but also a prostitute; yet the Lord honored her faith and courage in hiding the Hebrew spies.

This is an important reminder that the drastic action in destroying Jericho and its people is not God's final answer to human sin. His purpose is to save people, not destroy them. Howard wrote, "Christians should remember this in attempting to apply the principles of the *herem* to the modern day. While God abhors evil of every kind and Christians are to oppose it vigorously, the extremes of the *herem* are not enjoined upon Christians to practice today."[8]

❖ *Spiritual Transformations*

Because Jericho was a barrier to Israel's possessing the promised land, the Lord assured Joshua that He had given the city to them. Then He told Joshua what to tell the people about taking the city. The people carefully followed God's commands about marching around Jericho. The Lord commanded the Israelites to dedicate Jericho and all within it to Him by destroying people and possessions, saving only Rahab and her family and the valuable things of the city for the Lord's treasury. The Lord solemnly warned them against disobeying His commands and told them of the punishment for disobedience. When the people obeyed, the wall fell down and the Israelites easily took Jericho.

God's commands are to be taken seriously. We may not understand the reasons for some of God's commands, but we must obey even when we do not know all the reasons for His commands. Obedience and faith are two sides of the same coin. When we are willing to trust the Lord to do only what He can do, we show it by obeying His Word.

*Why does God not always explain to us the reasons He commands us to do something?*_____

What commands of the Lord are most difficult for you to obey? __

_____

Prayer of Commitment: Lord, I am grateful that although I cannot understand all Your ways and commands, You help me to act with trust and obedience.

[1]Howard, "Joshua," NAC, 173.

[2]Howard, "Joshua," NAC, 172.

[3]See the excursus in Howard, "Joshua," NAC, 180-187.

[4]Marten H. Woudstra, *The Book of Joshua,* in The New International Commentary on the Old Testament [Grand Rapids: William B. Eerdmans Publishing Company, 1981], 110.

[5]Zuck, *The Speaker's Quote Book,* 269.

[6]Howard, "Joshua," NAC, 173.

[7]Richard S. Hess, *Joshua,* in Tyndale Old Testament Commentaries [Downers Grove: Inter-Varsity Press, 1996], 134.

[8]Howard, "Joshua," NAC, 187.

Making a Commitment

Background Passage: Joshua 23:1–24:27
Focal Passage: Joshua 23:14; 24:14-27
Key Verse: Joshua 24:15

❖ *Significance of the Lesson*

• The *Theme* of this lesson is the Lord is God; people are to choose to serve and obey Him above all others.

• The *Life Question* this lesson seeks to address is, Whom will I choose to serve and obey?

• The *Biblical Theme* is that we should choose to serve and obey the Lord because of who He is and because of what He has done.

• The *Life Impact* is to help you serve the Lord above all others.

Serving God

Ours is a world of many cults and religions. People serve a variety of gods. Many claim to worship no god. According to many secular worldviews, one religion is as good as another; and for some worldviews, no religion is even better.

The biblical worldview is that everyone serves one god or another. People can choose their gods, but no one can choose not to choose. That to which we give our highest devotion is our god. The Bible insists that the only true God is the God and Father of our Lord Jesus Christ. He alone is worthy of worship and obedience.

Joshua's Two Final Addresses

Joshua 23 is often identified as Joshua's farewell address, while chapter 24 is recognized as a covenant renewal ceremony. Although there are similarities between the two chapters, each chapter has a distinctive emphasis. In both addresses Joshua called the people to remain faithful to the Lord. Chapter 23, however, emphasizes God's acts in the past, while chapter 24 includes what God will continue to do in the future.

Word Study: *Jealous*

The word "jealous" in 24:19 translates *qanno',* which is one of several related Hebrew words used to describe the demand by the Lord that He be the only God whom people worship and serve. One of the related words is found in the reasons for keeping the Second Commandment (see Ex. 20:5-6). God does not display the petty jealousies of the mythic, false pagan gods toward one another. His jealousy shows His demand for total allegiance and obedience.

❖ Search the Scriptures

In a farewell address, Joshua challenged the Israelites to fear and serve God with sincerity and truth. He called them to make a decision whether to serve the true God or some other god. When they promised to serve God, Joshua denied that they were able to do so, but they insisted that they could and would. Joshua made a covenant with them, and bound them to bear witness to their promise to serve God only.

The Challenge (Josh. 23:14; 24:14)

How does Joshua 23:14 emphasize the faithfulness of the Lord to Israel? How does Joshua 24:14 call for Israel to be faithful to the Lord? What is meant by the words **fear, serve, sincerity, truth***?*

23:14: And, behold, this day I am going the way of all the earth: and ye know in all your hearts and in all your souls, that not one thing hath failed of all the good things which the LORD your God spake concerning you; all are come to pass unto you, and not one thing hath failed thereof.

When Joshua was "old and stricken in age" (23:1-2), he called together the people and leaders of Israel. He reminded them how the Lord had given them the land (vv. 3-5). He challenged them to remain true to the law of Moses (v. 6). Joshua warned of failing to drive out the Canaanites (vv. 7-13). As for himself, Joshua said, **I am going the way of all the earth.** He was well aware that his life was about over. Since he was 110 when he died (24:29), this farewell address took place shortly before that time. His had been a long life; but most importantly, his life had been a life lived for God. Joshua tried to focus the people's attention on what the Lord had done for them.

The Lord had made many promises to Israel. Joshua said that they knew **in all** their **hearts and in all** their **souls** that **not one thing hath failed of all the good things which the** LORD their **God spake concerning** them. "Every promise has been fulfilled; not one has failed" (NIV). Joshua knew that the adults among them remembered the Lord's promises about crossing the Jordan, defeating the walled city of Jericho, and receiving the promised land. He was reminding them that God had kept every promise that He had made to them.

24:14: **Now therefore fear the** LORD, **and serve him in sincerity and in truth: and put away the gods which your fathers served on the other side of the flood, and in Egypt; and serve ye the** LORD.

Joshua called together at Shechem all the people and their leaders. He summarized the things the Lord had done from the time of Abraham until their own day. He showed how the Lord led Abraham from a family and culture that served many gods (24:3). Joshua gave a running account of the high points in the lives of Isaac, Jacob, and Moses (vv. 4-7). Joshua also talked about what God had done in the lifetimes of most of that adult generation, culminating in the gift of Canaan as their land (vv. 8-13).

Joshua's challenge to them began on this positive note: **Now therefore fear the** LORD, **and serve him in sincerity and in truth. Fear** and **serve** depict what they were to do toward the Lord. **Sincerity** and **truth** describe the spirit in which they were to act.

A number of words are used in the Old Testament to describe responses to the Lord. **Fear** and **serve** are used repeatedly. **Fear** is *yare'*. This word is often said to mean only a sense of reverence, and that is surely part of its meaning; however, **fear** also means to have a sense of awe in the presence of the holy God. Although the New Testament focuses on trusting the God of love, **fear** is still an appropriate response to God. Jesus said that believers should not fear what persecutors could do to them, but they should fear God (Matt. 10:28). Hebrews 10:31 says, "It is a fearful thing to fall into the hands of the living God." Hebrews 12:29 says, "Our God is a consuming fire." We should fear the consequences of disobeying the Lord.

Serve translates *'abad*. This word in some form appears 18 times in chapters 23–24. Seven of these are in 24:14-15. To **serve** God means to worship Him, to obey Him, to do whatever He asks us to do for Him. It is the Old Testament's all-purpose word for bringing together what God expects of His people. **Serve** can also be used of giving allegiance and obedience to false gods. Some people claim that the Lord is their God, but they actually have other gods to whom they give their service. They fear the Lord, but serve their own gods (2 Kings 17:33). Joshua and the entire Old Testament warn against this kind of hypocrisy.

Two words describe the spirit in which we are to **fear** and **serve** the Lord: **sincerity** and **truth. Sincerity** ("loyalty," NEB, REB) translates *tamim,* which means "wholeness," "perfection," "completeness," "blamelessness," and "integrity." Thus it includes the totality of our service. We are to be totally devoted in our service of God. **Truth** translates *'emet,* which has the idea of "faithfulness." Thus true fear and service to the Lord must be done with total commitment and faithfulness.

Put away ("throw away," NIV; "banish," NEB) indicates that some of the Israelites were serving other gods, just as their forefathers had done and just as their descendants would do. Verse 14 lists two categories (v. 15 will add a third and v. 23 a fourth). **Fathers** referred to their distant ancestors. These "forefathers" (NIV) are described in verse 2: "Your fathers dwelt on the other side of the flood in old time, even Terah, the father of Abraham, and the father of Nachor: and they served other gods." **The other side of the flood** ("beyond the River," NIV) here refers to the Euphrates River. This shows that Abraham came out of a country and even a family that served other gods. We can see evidences that this continued after Terah's family moved to Haran. Jacob's uncle Laban had such gods, and even Jacob's beloved wife Rachel seems to have done the same (Gen. 31:19,30-32). Jacob's children had some such gods (35:2). **In Egypt** the Israelites had worshiped false gods (see Lev. 17:7; Deut. 32:16-17).

Most of us wonder what was the appeal of worshiping man-made idols of wood and stone. The appeal was in the promises of these gods and in the amoral demands on the worshipers. An idol can be manipulated to ask for whatever the worshiper wants. The Old Testament revelation of God challenged idol worshipers at two basic points. Ethical monotheism insists that there is only one God and that He is a holy God who demands that His people be holy. If there are many gods, people cannot give total service to any one of them. If there is only one God, total commitment can be given to Him.

Likewise, people today have their own gods. Our gods are whatever we give our highest allegiance to and that in which we place our greatest trust. In *A Christmas Carol,* Charles Dickens tells how the Spirit of Christmas Past forced Scrooge to recall his last meeting with the young woman to whom he earlier had promised his love. She told him: "Another idol has displaced me; and if it can cheer and comfort you in time to come, as I would have tried to do, I have no just cause to grieve."[1] The other idol was Scrooge's obsession with wealth. Many in our day worship this same god. Whatever receives our greatest attention, in which we place our trust, is our god.

The Options (Josh. 24:15)

*What third category of gods did Joshua mention? How could Joshua speak for himself and for his **house**? Why does the Bible teach that we must **choose**? Why is the demand that we choose **this day**?*

24:15: And if it seem evil unto you to serve the LORD, choose you this day whom ye will serve; whether the gods which your fathers served that were on the other side of the flood, or the gods of the Amorites, in whose land ye dwell: but as for me and my house, we will serve the LORD.

This is one of the great verses in the Bible. Probably more sermons have been preached on this verse than any other in the Book of Joshua. **And if it seem evil** ("undesirable," NIV; "disagreeable," NASB) is literally "is evil in your eyes." Some translations have used words that are more common today: "if you are unwilling" (NRSV) and "if it does not please you" (NEB, REB).

Choose is often used in the Old Testament to describe God's choice of Israel to be His people. Here Joshua used it to describe the choice Israel needed to make to be the people God called them to be. This shows that human choice is involved in having a right relation with God. They were free to choose God or some other god, but they must live and die with the consequences of their choice.

There are two important biblical truths about this most crucial of human choices. One is that we are free to choose our god, but we are not free not to choose. Many people today claim they are neutral— that they are free and unshackled by allegiance to any god. They are wrong. As humans, we are free to choose our gods, but we are not free not to choose. If we choose not to serve the Lord, we end up with some other god—whether we recognize it or not. Second, this call to choose between God or some other god shows that we cannot serve God and any other god. Jesus said, "No man can serve two masters: for either he will hate the one, and love the other; or else he will hold to the one, and despise the other. Ye cannot serve God and mammon" (Matt. 6:24). God demands our total devotion and service.

This day shows the urgency of the choice. Joshua knew this was his last opportunity to call them to commitment. He also knew that only with total commitment could they settle in Canaan without yielding to the temptations of the land.

Joshua added a third category of false gods to the two categories in verse 14. They were not to serve **the gods of the Amorites** in the land of Canaan. **Amorites** is used here in the general sense of Canaanites. The chief religion of Canaan was Baal worship. The Israelites had already had a serious outbreak of this kind of worship (see Num. 25). Baal worship appealed to the Israelites in two ways: It was a fertility religion that promised bountiful crops, and it included sexual immorality as part of its worship.

Joshua made his own commitment clear. He declared, **As for me and my house, we will serve the Lord.** "Joshua took his stand clearly and unambiguously on the Lord's side. Joshua stands as a good example of a leader willing to move ahead of his people and commit himself, regardless of the people's inclinations."[2] He committed himself completely. His life had been one of total commitment. He also included his **house** ("household," NIV) or family. No father can guarantee that his family will follow his commitment, but a committed father has great influence in the religious leadership of his family.

Joshua's challenge has much in common with some of the other Bible calls to commitment. For example, after the Israelites made the golden calf, Moses said, "Who is on the Lord's side? let him come unto me" (Ex. 32:26). Also, remember the choice placed before the Israelites by Elijah, "How long halt ye between two opinions? if the Lord be God, follow him: but if Baal, then follow him" (1 Kings 18:21). Moses, Joshua, and Elijah did not acknowledge the reality of the false gods, but each knew that the people were placing their trust in gods that could not truly help them. Only the Lord is able to fill the God-shaped emptiness in each human heart.

The Choice (Josh. 24:16-24)

What was the response of the people to Joshua's challenge? Why did Joshua say they were not able to serve the Lord? How did they respond to his words?

24:16-18: **And the people answered and said, God forbid that we should forsake the Lord, to serve other gods; [17]for the Lord our God, he it is that brought us up and our fathers out of the land of Egypt, from the house of bondage, and which did those great signs in our sight, and preserved us in all the way wherein we went, and among all the people through whom we passed: [18]and the Lord drove out from before us all the people, even the Amorites which dwelt in the land: therefore will we also serve the Lord; for he is our God.**

God forbid is "far be it from us" (NIV, NKJV). They denied they would ever **forsake the Lord, to serve other gods.** Then they gave their own testimony of the past deliverances and blessings they and their fathers had received from the Lord. Joshua had done this in verses 2-13. The people acknowledged it was **the Lord** their **God** who **brought** them **out of the land of Egypt.** They said they were in **bondage** and incapable of escaping or defeating their oppressors. But God did what they could not do. He used **great signs** to deliver them. He also **preserved** them in the wilderness, giving them a way to pass **through** pagan nations on their way to Canaan.

Then within the recent past, **the Lord drove out** the people of the land of Canaan. Thus the Israelites responded to Joshua's call for commitment by declaring, **Therefore will we also serve the Lord; for he is our God.**

24:19-20: **And Joshua said unto the people, Ye cannot serve the Lord: for he is an holy God; he is a jealous God; he will not forgive your transgressions nor your sins. [20]If ye forsake the Lord, and serve strange gods, then he will turn and do you hurt, and consume you, after that he hath done you good.**

Joshua's response must have stunned the people. After their profession of faith, **Joshua said unto the people, Ye cannot** ("are not able to," NIV) **serve the Lord.** He explained they were not able to do this because God is **holy** and **jealous.** These two characteristics grow out of God's revelation of Himself as the one and only God, who expects total devotion from His people. This religion is called ethical monotheism. It differed in two important ways from pagan religions, which were amoral or immoral polytheism. That is, they worshiped many gods, and these gods made no moral demands on them; in fact, many of the gods were used to promoted immorality. Because God is **holy,** He expects His people to be holy. The word **holy** means "to be set apart." In the same way, God is **jealous** because He is the only God. He fits into only one place in human devotion. Either we give our all out of devotion to Him, or we give none. God will not accept less than total devotion.

Joshua continued, **He will not forgive your transgressions nor your sins.** This statement seems to deny the revelation in Exodus 34:6-7. This does not deny that the Lord is merciful and gracious to repentant sinners, but it does affirm that He will by no means clear the guilty. That is, He will **not forgive** those who persist in rebellion and sin.

This warning is to those who **forsake the LORD, and serve strange** ("foreign," NIV) **gods.** Instead, Joshua warned, God **will turn and do you hurt, and consume you** ("he will turn and bring disaster on you and make an end of you," NIV). This warning was to those to whom the Lord had done **good,** but who forsook the Lord for other gods.

Joshua no doubt was thinking of the past record of their fathers. They repeatedly had rebelled. After the covenant was offered to them at Mount Sinai, they promised, "All that the Lord hath spoken we will do" (Ex. 19:8), but shortly after this commitment they made the golden calf. Joshua spoke hard words not to discourage them but to ensure that any commitment they made was made in full awareness of the cost.

24:21-24: **And the people said unto Joshua, Nay; but we will serve the LORD.** [22]**And Joshua said unto the people, Ye are witnesses against yourselves that ye have chosen you the LORD, to serve him. And they said, We are witnesses.** [23]**Now therefore put away, said he, the strange gods which are among you, and incline your heart unto the LORD God of Israel.** [24]**And the people said unto Joshua, The LORD our God will we serve, and his voice will we obey.**

The people were quick to deny these charges, declaring, **Nay; but we will serve the LORD.** Joshua was equally quick to come back with these words: **Ye are witnesses against yourselves that ye have chosen you the LORD, to serve him.** They were their own witnesses to their promises. And they agreed, **We are witnesses.**

Then Joshua told them to **put away** a fourth category of **strange gods.** He was referring to the gods that were **among** them. In other words, some of them had brought false gods with them and had them in their homes in shrines. They needed to get rid of these.

Joshua continued to appeal to them, saying, **Incline** ("yield," NIV) **your heart unto the LORD God of Israel.** The people once again affirmed their commitment: **The LORD our God will we serve, and his voice will we obey.** The test of this commitment would be their long-range actions.

The Accountability (Josh. 24:25-27)

*Did Joshua renew the existing covenant or make a new one? What was **the book of the law of God**? What was **the sanctuary of the Lord**? What was the purpose of the **stone**?*

24:25-27: So Joshua made a covenant with the people that day, and set them a statute and an ordinance in Shechem. ²⁶And Joshua wrote these words in the book of the law of God, and took a great stone, and set it up there under an oak, that was by the sanctuary of the Lord. ²⁷And Joshua said unto all the people, Behold, this stone shall be a witness unto us; for it hath heard all the words of the Lord which he spake unto us: it shall be therefore a witness unto you, lest ye deny your God.

The **covenant** that Joshua made with them seems to have been a renewal of the covenant from Mount Sinai. During the early part of the campaign in Canaan, Joshua led them in renewing the covenant at Mount Ebal and Mount Gerizim (8:30-35). Now that the land was mostly in Israelite hands, Joshua led them in another renewal. The abiding truth is that all people need to renew their vows with the Lord from time to time. Our relationship with God is not something we do only once. We enter it at one time and place, but if the relationship is real, like all personal relationships, it must be renewed from time to time. The process of covenant renewals included reviewing what the Lord had done for them and renewing their commitments to the Lord.

We don't know exactly what **the book of the law of God** was in which **Joshua wrote these words,** but David Howard reminded us that "the essence of its contents is known to us via the present canonical Book of Joshua."[3] Then Joshua **took a great stone, and set it up there under an oak, that was by the sanctuary of the Lord.** The **stone** was to serve as **a witness** unto them. The stone itself had **heard all the words of the Lord which he spake unto** them. The stone had also been a silent witness to their words of commitment. It was set up near the tabernacle, so that people would see it when they came to worship and would be reminded of the Lord's works and of their total commitment to serve Him.

By hearing the words of the Lord and committing themselves to Him, the people became accountable to maintain their commitment. Nevertheless, Joshua spoke of the stone as if **it** had heard all that was said on that day. Therefore, if they forsook the Lord, the stone would be one of the witnesses to remind them of their commitments, and thus to condemn them for failing to remain true to the Lord. The stone was to serve as a warning against denying the Lord, whom they had promised to serve.

Verses 29-30 tell of Joshua's death and burial. Verse 31 tells of his amazing influence: "Israel served the Lord all the days of Joshua, and all the days of the elders that outlived Joshua, and which had known all the works of the Lord, that he had done for Israel." This is an amazing testimony and tribute to the man Joshua. His total commitment led others to make or to renew their own covenants with the Lord. Only great people influence their own generation for God and good. Even greater people influence not only their own generation but also the following one. This illustrates the power of total commitment to God in one's life.

❖ *Spiritual Transformations*

Joshua issued a challenge for Israel to be as faithful to the Lord as He had been to them. He called for them to make a total commitment, and he stated publicly his total commitment. When they promised to serve the Lord only, Joshua challenged them by denying they could do this. This led them to make another statement of their commitment. Then Joshua renewed God's covenant with them.

The applications of the four points in the outline are these: (1) God calls people to total commitment to Him. (2) Each person is free to choose or to reject the Lord, but none of us is free not to choose some god or other. (3) A genuine commitment is not short-lived but lasting. (4) Our commitment to the Lord needs to be renewed from time to time.

The impact of this lesson on our lives should be to call us to make a first-time commitment or a renewed commitment to serve the Lord totally and faithfully.

Have you made a commitment to the Lord? _____

When and how do you renew your commitment to the Lord? _____

_____

How does your commitment compare to Joshua's? _____

Prayer of Commitment: Lord, help me to serve You totally and faithfully. Amen.

[1]Charles Dickens, *A Christmas Carol* [New York: Washington Square Press, 1939], 89.
[2]Howard, "Joshua," NAC, 436.
[3]Howard, "Joshua," NAC, 440.

Study Theme

God's Plan for Families

While teaching a class of older children, the teacher asked two questions: "If you could choose, where had you rather be than anywhere else? Where had you rather not be?" In answering the second question, one of the boys said, "I'd rather be anywhere than at home!" The teacher had been in the child's home and understood why he said what he did. Although his parents were professing Christians and church members, their home life showed little evidence of it.

Christian families are under attack today. Many people question biblical faith and morals. Christians need to base their beliefs and behaviors on the teachings of God's Word. What does the Bible teach about God's plan for families? This unit of four lessons will focus on four aspects of biblical teachings about the family. Studies will explore Bible passages that uplift the family as the center of biblical guidance, the Bible as the basis of spiritual instruction, the church as a partner with the family in teaching and ministry, and the good news of Jesus Christ as the message families are to share with non-Christian individuals and families.

The study theme is designed to help you—

• make your family a center of biblical instruction and guidance for your family members (Oct. 7)

• emphasize and use the Bible as the primary source of moral and religious instruction in your family (Oct. 14)

• be involved in your church's educational and ministry programs so your family can learn more about God and serve Him better (Oct. 21)

• lead your family to share the good news of Christ with others (Oct. 28)

The Bible passages for the first lesson come from Deuteronomy. The second lesson uses Bible passages from Acts and 2 Timothy to focus on Timothy's training and service. Passages from Titus are the biblical basis for the third lesson. The fourth lesson is based on the biblical account of Peter and Cornelius in Acts 10.

In what ways does your family show evidence that you are a Christian family? _____

The Home: The Center of Biblical Guidance

Background Passage: Deuteronomy 4:9-14; 6:1-25
Focal Passage: Deuteronomy 4:9-10; 6:1-7,20-25
Key Verses: Deuteronomy 6:6-7

❖ *Significance of the Lesson*

• The *Theme* of this lesson is that the home is the primary center for biblical instruction and guidance.

• The *Life Question* this lesson seeks to address is, Why should I make my home the primary center of biblical instruction for my family?

• The *Biblical Truth* is that God's people are to teach their children His directives for living.

• The *Life Impact* is to help you make your family a center of biblical instruction and guidance for your family members.

Worldviews About Teaching Religion in the Home

Adults who hold to secular worldviews have no vital religious faith to share with their children or grandchildren. Thus in such homes little moral values are taught and no spiritual guidelines are offered. Parents sometimes say they don't want to force any religion on their children but leave them to make their own decisions. In this so-called neutral environment, the children learn their values from television and peer groups.

According to the biblical worldview, the family has the strategic role in teaching Christian values and beliefs. The ideal is for parents to teach their children through instruction and consistent living. Many Christian parents struggle to find time to do this.

Word Study: *Teach . . . diligently*

Several different Hebrew words are translated *teach.* The word in Deuteronomy 6:7 is *sanan*, which most think means "sharpen" or "impress" (NIV). A parent is to "impress the words of covenant faith into the thinking of his children by inscribing them there with indelible sharpness and precision."[1] Some Bible students think *sanan* means "repeat," thus supporting the teaching-learning method of repetition.

❖ *Search the Scriptures*

God spoke through Moses to command the Israelites to teach their children and grandchildren. One expression of this was teaching their children formally and informally. Parents were taught to seize the teachable moments that came when their children asked questions.

Command to Teach (Deut. 4:9-10)

*What key themes of the Book of Deuteronomy are found in 4:9-10? What were the people warned not to forget? What are the meanings of the two words for **teach**? What were the **words** in verse 10? Why did God command parents to teach their children? How can grandparents teach their grandchildren in today's society?*

4:9-10: Only take heed to thyself, and keep thy soul diligently, lest thou forget the things which thine eyes have seen, and lest they depart from thy heart all the days of thy life: but teach them thy sons, and thy sons' sons; [10]**specially the day that thou stoodest before the LORD thy God in Horeb, when the LORD said unto me, Gather me the people together, and I will make them hear my words, that they may learn to fear me all the days that they shall live upon the earth, and that they may teach their children.**

Moses' first sermon was Deuteronomy 1–4. Chapters 1–3 gives a summary of what the Lord had done for Israel, beginning with the deliverance from Egypt. Chapter 4 is an exhortation to them about what they should do in response to what God had done for them.

Many of the basic themes of Deuteronomy are in verses 9-10. One theme is the warning against forgetting, which often is stated positively as "remember." The use of italics in printed editions of the *King James Version* indicates the words were not in the Hebrew but were added by translators to clarify the meaning. **Specially** at the beginning of verse 10 is such an addition. Some translations add "remember" (NIV, NASB). The word *remember* is a key word in the book, being found 13 times.

Forget (*sakah*) is used in 4:9 and is found 11 times in Deuteronomy (in the KJV) in warnings against forgetting the Lord and what He had done for them. Sometimes the words *remember* and *forget* occur in the same verse (see 9:7). Moses told the people to **take heed to thyself, and keep thy soul diligently** with full awareness that forgetting is a danger to avoid. The sin of forgetting would let God's truth **depart** ("slip," NIV) **from** their hearts.

The Book of Deuteronomy warns against forgetting **things** that their **eyes** had **seen** when God delivered Israel from Egypt. Moses was speaking mostly to second-generation Israelites. The only ones of this group who were alive at the time of the exodus were the adults who were now over 40. They had been children or teenagers at the time of the exodus. However, Moses spoke to all of the people as if they personally had witnessed the deliverance from Egypt and the covenant at **Horeb** (another name for Mount Sinai). The sense of continuity from one generation to another was so strong that it was as if they personally had been there. During the 40 years in the wilderness, the second generation who had no memories of the event had heard of these things.

They in turn were told to **teach** ("make them known," NASB) these same things to their **sons** and to their **sons' sons** ("to your children and to their children after them," NIV; "to your children and your grandchildren," NKJV). The word for **teach** in verse 9 is *yada'*, which means "to cause to know." The word for **teach** in verse 10 is *lamed*, which means "to teach," "to instruct," "to train." The responsibility for teaching was thus given to parents, especially to fathers. When a man's children were growing up, he was to teach them; when his grandchildren were born, he shared with his grown son the responsibility for teaching the grandchildren. In verse 10, the **words** they heard at **Horeb** seem to have been the Ten Commandments. At least they were what are mentioned in 4:13.

Parents use various excuses for not teaching their children about God. Some say that religion was forced on them and they resolved not to force it on their children. Many say they would like to teach their children, but they are too busy to find time.

Parents need to realize several facts. For one thing, all parents teach their children something about God. It may be that they are teaching that God is not important, since the parents live without God. For another thing, no child grows up in a neutral environment. Samuel Taylor Coleridge, the great English poet, was talking with a man who did not believe in giving children religious training. His argument was that the child should not be prejudiced either for or against religion but grow up before he made any decision. Coleridge invited the man to look at his garden. When the man saw the garden, he said, "Why, this is not a garden! There are nothing but weeds here!" Coleridge replied, "Well, you see, I did not want to infringe upon the liberty of the garden in any way. I was just giving the garden a chance to express itself and to choose its own production."[2]

Children do not grow up in a neutral environment. They are subjected to all kinds of evil influences. They deserve to have an opportunity to know and serve God. This opportunity ought to take place in the home. That is a command of God.

Grandparents in today's society may have problems seeking to teach their grandchildren. Often the grandchildren live far away. Sometimes the parents resent the grandparents teaching their children. There are no easy answers to the dilemma of believing grandparents whose grown children are not teaching the grandchildren about God and who consider any attempt to do so as interference.

Purpose of Teaching (Deut. 6:1-3,24-25)

Who is the teacher in 6:1? What was the content of the teaching? What responses were supposed to be made to the teaching? What were the desired end-results of the teaching?

6:1-3: Now these are the commandments, the statutes, and the judgments, which the Lord your God commanded to teach you, that ye might do them in the land whither ye go to possess it: ²that thou mightest fear the Lord thy God, to keep all his statutes and his commandments, which I command thee, thou, and thy son, and thy son's son, all the days of thy life; and that thy days may be prolonged. ³Hear therefore, O Israel, and observe to do it; that it may be well with thee, and that ye may increase mightily, as the Lord God of thy fathers hath promised thee, in the land that floweth with milk and honey.

The Lord . . . commanded Moses to **teach** the people. The Lord taught Moses, who then taught the people. They in turn were to teach their children. Moses was to teach **the commandments, the statutes, and the judgments.** Deuteronomy 4:13 said for them to teach the Ten Commandments, but 5:1 seems to refer to the multitude of specific regulations that are found beginning in Deuteronomy 12:1.

Several words describe the desired response of the people to the Lord's teaching through Moses. **Fear** often is used in the Old

Testament to describe how people should respond to the Lord and His commandments. **Keep** and **observe** describe what those who fear the Lord do with the commandments of the Lord. As in 4:9, the ones to be influenced by the teachings were their **son and** their **son's son** ("your son and your grandson," NKJV). This was essential if the faith was to be passed on. Each generation must teach the next generation. If they fail, we are always a generation or no more than two generations away from paganism. The Lord taught Moses, who in turn taught the people. The next link in the chain was for the father to teach his son, then for the son to teach his son.

Unfortunately, what often happens is that the second generation never shares the total commitment of their parents. Thus theirs is a nominal faith and a compromised life. Their children see nothing appealing in the shallow profession and inconsistent lives of their parents. Thus they reject such a religion. Bruce H. Wilkinson in his book *The Three Chairs: Experiencing Spiritual Breakthroughs* characterized a first generation of believers as one based on commitment, a second generation of nominal believers as one living with compromise, and a third generation without faith as one steeped in conflict.[3]

For those who had a vital faith that was effectively shared with their children, God made several promises. They would live a long **(thy days may be prolonged)** and good **(it may be well with thee)** life in a **land** flowing **with milk and honey.** This analogy for the richness of the land of promise was often used in the Bible. It is found four times in Exodus, once in Leviticus, four times in Numbers, and six times in Deuteronomy. "The phrase 'milk and 'honey' is a hyperbolic way of describing the richness of the land of promise. These two commodities, the one the product of human labor, or agriculture, the other the product of nature, represent the fullness of blessing associated with the fulfillment of God's promises."[4]

6:24-25: And the LORD commanded us to do all these statutes, to fear the LORD our God, for our good always, that he might preserve us alive, as it is at this day. [25]And it shall be our righteousness, if we observe to do all these commandments before the LORD our God, as he hath commanded us.

Deuteronomy 6 ends with the same themes with which it begins. The Lord promised to those who **fear** Him the **good** life. This involved entry into the promised land, where they would live long and prosper; but their greatest treasure was their relationship with the Lord.

Righteousness would be one result of obeying the Lord's commandments. Eugene Merrill noted: "The word used here is *sedaqa*, the very one applied to Abraham as a result of his having believed in the Lord (Gen. 15:6). Later Judaism wrongly concluded that covenant keeping was the basis for righteousness rather than an expression of faithful devotion. But true covenant keeping in the final analysis is a matter of faith, not merely of works and ritual. Thus the central feature of the covenant stipulations is their providing a vehicle by which genuine saving faith might be displayed (cf. Deut. 24:13; Hab. 2:4; Rom. 1:17; 4:1-5; Gal. 3:6-7)."[5]

Many people think of God as the ultimate killjoy. That is, they think that the commandments of the Lord remove the joys of life. Such people often describe the life they seek as "the good life." Faith and obedience to God is the last place they would expect to find the good life. They seek the good life in worldly things. Believers can bear witness to the biblical truth that the truly good life is found only in total obedience to the Lord.

Most parents want their children to have a good life. Too many of these parents define this good life in materialistic terms. However, along with the physical things needed to sustain life, children need moral and spiritual things. Parents are accountable for providing the spiritual things of the truly good life.

Contexts for Teaching (Deut. 6:4-7)

What is the Shema*? Why is verse 5 called the greatest commandment? What does having this commandment on one's heart mean? Why is verse 7 considered by some to be the most important words to parents in the Bible?*

6:4-5: Hear, O Israel: the Lord our God is one Lord: [5]and thou shalt love the Lord thy God with all thine heart, and with all thy soul, and with all thy might.

Many Jews recite a daily prayer that usually includes verses 4-5, often includes verses 6-9, and sometimes includes Deuteronomy 11:13-21 and Numbers 15:37-41. This is called the Shema, from the first word of Deuteronomy 6:4 in the Hebrew text, the imperative of the verb for "hear." Jesus taught that these verses constitute the greatest commandment of the law (Matt. 22:37-38; see also Mark 12:29-30 and Luke 10:27-28).

Verse 4 is a basic confession of faith in God. "This central confession of faith consists of only four words [in Hebrew], *Yahweh, our God, Yahweh, One.* The expression has been variously understood. Possible translations are 'Yahweh our God, Yahweh is one.' 'Yahweh is our God, Yahweh is one.' 'Yahweh is our God, Yahweh alone.' Whatever translation is chosen the essential meaning is clear. Yahweh was to be the sole object of Israel's worship, allegiance, and affection."[6]

These words emphasize the unity and uniqueness of the Lord God. Jesus and the apostles were loyal to the basic belief in the one God. They also taught that His oneness did not mean God is restricted to human understandings of *one.* The one God has revealed Himself as Father, Son, and Holy Spirit. This is also how Christians have experienced Him.

The word **love** is not the usual word in the Old Testament for the appropriate human response to God. Words such as *fear, obey, worship, serve, worship, praise,* and *trust* are more familiar. However, in verse 5, **love** is used to describe the basic response to God. The word is closely related to *obey.* On the other hand, **love** is a family word, which implies an allegiance that goes beyond obedience to a commandment.

All is the key word in the last part of verse 5. Reference to **heart . . . soul . . . might** was not intended to divide a person into components; instead, the point is that we are to love the Lord with all that we have and are. Every part of our mind, feelings, will, abilities, time, and energy is to focus on the one God, who is our Lord. If someone truly believes in one God, the only appropriate response is wholehearted love. People who worship more than one god cannot do this because they must spread their love between their gods.

6:6-7: And these words, which I command thee this day, shall be in thine heart: [7]and thou shalt teach them diligently unto thy children, and shalt talk of them when thou sittest in thine house, and when thou walkest by the way, and when thou liest down, and when thou risest up.

Here are two related actions for those who love the Lord wholeheartedly. For one thing, each person is to integrate **these words** into his or her total being. That is, they are to be **in thine heart.** This means several things about the people who do this. They have a personal relationship with the Lord because of His love for them and their love for Him. It also means they know these words. They have memorized them, and they have obeyed them. This kind of love must be one's conscious, constant reflection (see vv. 8-9).

This first step is necessary for parents to be able to fulfill the second action described in verse 7—to **teach** these words to their **children. Teach . . . diligently** uses a different word for *teach* than either of the words in 4:9-10. There are three schools of thought about the meaning of the Hebrew word: Some translate it as **teach . . . diligently.** Others prefer "impress" (NIV). Still others use "repeat" (NEB) or "recite" (NRSV). All three translations emphasize the responsibility of believing parents to pass along the faith to their children.

James C. Dobson wrote of Deuteronomy 6:6-9: "I believe this commandment from the Lord is one of the most crucial verses for parents in the entire Bible. It instructs us to surround our children with godly teaching. References to spiritual things are not to be reserved just for Sunday morning or even for a bedtime prayer. They should permeate our conversation and the fabric of our lives."[7]

How are believing parents to fulfill this important duty? Verse 7 makes several assumptions about how to do this. One is that faith and obedience are real to the parents. Their children will hear only parents who live their faith. No one knows us better than the members of our own family. When a growing child sees his father and mother living differently at home than they do at church, the child often rejects such religion.

Second is that both formal and informal religious training are important. The emphasis here is on informal teaching as opportunities occur. Such teachings are woven into the fabric of daily life. The parents are to **talk** about the things of the Lord as they go about the routines of daily life **(when thou sittest in thine house)** and as they travel outside **(when thou walkest by the way).** Believing parents also talk about the things of God as they put the children down for the night **(when thou liest down)** and at the beginning of a new day **(when thou riseth up).**

Third is that the parents spend time with their children. The verse speaks of being at home, traveling, night, and morning. These parents spent time with their children. Many Christian parents spend little time with their children. Often both parents work outside the home, and they are too tired or busy to be with their children in any meaningful way.

Fourth is that children grow up quickly and parents have only a narrow time when the hearts of their children are open to teachings (see Prov. 22:6). When their children are born, parents often think of having them for a long time; but ask any parent whose children have grown up. They will tell you that your time with them is precious and moves quickly away.

Concerning methods of instruction, daily conversations are stressed. Repeating basic truths is essential for learning. Memorization is used.

Deuteronomy 6:7 is the motto of the Family Bible Study Series, which includes materials for each age group that are designed not only for Sunday Bible study but also for family Bible study. Won't you take full advantage of the suggestions in the quarterlies for your family?

Teachable Moments (Deut. 6:20-23)

How can parents recognize teachable moments? How can they help create teachable moments? Why should parents not be intimidated by questions their children ask about God and the Bible? How are stories an important way to teach children?

6:20-23: And when thy son asketh thee in time to come, saying, What mean the testimonies, and the statutes, and the judgments, which the Lord our God hath commanded you? [21]Then thou shalt say unto thy son, We were Pharaoh's bondmen in Egypt; and the Lord brought us out of Egypt with a mighty hand: [22]and the Lord showed signs and wonders, great and sore, upon Egypt, upon Pharaoh, and upon all his household, before our eyes: [23]and he brought us out from thence, that he might bring us in, to give us the land which he sware unto our fathers.

The contents of the parents' teaching included the Ten Commandments, the Shema, and other commandments of the Lord. Children heard their parents reciting these or reading them. This led perceptive and curious children to ask **what** these things **mean.** Such questions provide excellent teachable moments.

Bible stories are an excellent way to teach children the Bible. This is essentially how Moses told the people of Israel to answer their children's questions. Verses 21-23 tell the story of what God had done in the lives of their ancestors. The Israelites were slaves in Egypt when **the Lord brought** them **out of Egypt with a mighty hand.** He did that by using **signs and wonders.** Parents could say to their children, **He brought us out from thence, that he might bring us in, to give us the land which he sware unto our fathers.** Notice that Moses used **we** and **us** to describe those who were delivered. In other words, the deliverance of their forefathers was tantamount to delivering each generation of believing Israelites.

Family and church observances provide modern parents with teachable moments. Witnessing a baptism or watching church members observe the Lord's Supper often lead to questions from small children. The answers parents give can focus on the heart of the Christian gospel, in terms suited to the age and maturity of the child.

❖ *Spiritual Transformations*

Moses told the Israelites to teach their children and grandchildren what God had done for Israel and what He expected of them. God taught Moses to tell the people that obedience would lead them to enjoy the good life God wanted to give them. He summarized Israel's faith in the one God and their need to love God with all their being. He commanded parents to impress these things on their children early and late, coming or going. Moses encouraged the parents to answer questions that their children asked.

Each generation of believers must pass on the faith to the next generation. The primary responsibility for this is given to parents. Christian parents are responsible for formal and informal teaching of their children. To do this, the parents themselves must be committed believers who practice what they teach. Many modern parents are so busy that they neglect this basic duty.

*How can busy parents find the time to teach their children biblical truths?*_____

How can parents create teachable moments to teach their children?

_____

*How can grandparents help teach their grandchildren?*_____

_____

Prayer of Commitment: Lord, teach me Your ways, and help me teach the next generation Your Word.

[1]Eugene H. Merrill, "Deuteronomy," in *The New American Commentary*, vol. 4 [Nashville: Broadman & Holman Publishers, 1994], 167.

[2]Zuck, *The Speaker's Quote Book*, 51-52.

[3]Bruce H. Wilkinson, *The Three Chairs: Experiencing Spiritual Breakthroughs* [Nashville: LifeWay Press, 1999], 13.

[4]Merrill, "Deuteronomy," NAC, 161.

[5]Merrill, "Deuteronomy," NAC, 175.

[6]J. A. Thompson, *Deuteronomy*, in the Tyndale Old Testament Commentaries [Downers Grove: InterVarsity Press, 1974], 121.

[7]James C. Dobson, *Parenting Isn't for Cowards* [Waco: Word Books Publisher, 1987], 106.

The Bible: The Family's Source of Instruction

Background Passage: Acts 16:1-5; 2 Timothy 1:3-7; 3:10–4:5
Focal Passage: Acts 16:1-5; 2 Timothy 1:5-6; 3:14–4:5
Key Verses: 2 Timothy 3:15-16

❖ *Significance of the Lesson*

• The *Theme* of this lesson is that the Bible, God's Word, is the family's source of instruction and guidance for what we should believe and how we should behave.

• The *Life Question* this lesson seeks to address is, What role does the Bible play in my family?

• The *Biblical Truth* is that the Bible is God's inspired Word and is the source for life's most important teaching; parents are to teach their children truths from the Bible.

• The *Life Impact* is to help you emphasize and use the Bible as the primary source of moral and religious instruction in your family.

The Place of the Bible in the Home

Some families do not even have a Bible in their homes. Others have one or more Bibles, but they gather dust from not being used. Many things are taught in a secular home—some deliberately and others by default—but the Bible is not among the sources from which people are taught and its values are not something by which they live. The secular culture through its media is a powerful influence. The result is an education designed to achieve success measured by the world's standards, to accumulate material possessions, and to assure personal security, even at others' expense.

The biblical worldview recognizes the Bible as God's authoritative Word. The Bible points to the way of salvation, and it shapes beliefs and behavior according to God's pattern. Thus the Bible is to be the primary source of moral and religious instruction not only in the church but also in believers' families. Children ought to be taught the Bible by their parents.

Word Study: *Holy Scriptures*

The Bible uses many words to describe itself. One of the most common of these is *graphe*, or "Scripture," in 2 Timothy 3:16. In verse 15 two words are used, *hiera grammata*, which is literally "sacred writings" (NASB, NRSV). This is the only use of this combination in the New Testament. Josephus, the first-century Jewish historian, used the words to refer to the Old Testament. This plus the fact that they are used along with *graphe* in this passage show that the expression means the "holy Scriptures."

❖ *Search the Scriptures*

Paul chose Timothy, a highly respected young Christian from Lystra, to go with him as a fellow worker. Timothy's faith was strongly influenced by the faith and Bible teachings of his mother and grandmother. Paul spoke of every Scripture as "God-breathed." The Word of God leads people to faith in Christ and instructs them in Christian beliefs and behavior. As a leader in the church, Timothy was to preach the Word.

A Mother's Influence (Acts 16:1-5)

What people influenced Timothy to become a Christian and to grow in faith? When was his mother converted? In what sense did he grow up in a home with a mixed marriage? What role did Paul play in Timothy's conversion? Why did Paul have Timothy circumcised? Why did Paul select Timothy to go with him? What people most influenced you in becoming a Christian and finding God's will?

Acts 16:1-5: Then came he to Derbe and Lystra: and, behold, a certain disciple was there, named Timotheus, the son of a certain woman, which was a Jewess, and believed; but his father was a Greek: [2]which was well reported of by the brethren that were at Lystra and Iconium. [3]Him would Paul have to go forth with him; and took and circumcised him because of the Jews which were in those quarters: for they knew all that his father was a Greek. [4]And as they went through the cities, they delivered them the decrees for to keep, that were ordained of the apostles and elders which were at Jerusalem. [5]And so were the churches established in the faith, and increased in number daily.

On Paul's first missionary journey he and Barnabas had preached the good news in the towns of Iconium, Lystra, and Derbe in the south central part of Asia Minor. Although Paul was persecuted in each town, and almost killed at least once, he went back through them to encourage the believers in the newly established churches (Acts 14: 1-28). On the second missionary journey, Paul and Silas returned to **Derbe** and to **Lystra.** On the first journey, he was traveling from west to east; on the second, he was traveling from east to west.

In one of these towns, probably Lystra, lived **Timotheus,** that is, Timothy, **the son of a certain woman, which was a Jewess, and believed; but his father was a Greek.** This tells us several important facts about Timothy. For one thing, he was a child of a mixed marriage as far as religion was concerned. Timothy's mother was Jewish and also a Christian believer. His father was a Greek. The way his father is described implies that he was not a believer in God or a Christian. Some Bible students think the wording implies that his father was dead. At any rate, he had not been a positive influence on the religious life of his son. Since Timothy was not circumcised, this may indicate that his father had objected to his becoming a believer. It surely means that his father was not a positive influence in the home, and possibly he was a negative one. Timothy's mother thus was one of many believing women who have had to provide the primary moral and spiritual training for her child.

When did Timothy's mother believe in Jesus? The most likely time was during Paul's first visit to their town. Second Timothy 1:5 implies that she believed before Timothy. It is likely that Timothy also was converted during Paul's first visit. Paul's many references to Timothy as his son in the faith imply that Paul played a primary role in Timothy's conversion, probably winning him to the Lord. However, this does not overshadow the crucial role played by Timothy's mother in bringing him up—to the extent that she could—in the faith of the Old Testament.

Verse 2 shows that by the time of Paul's second missionary journey Timothy had been a Christian long enough to be noticed **by the brethren that were at Lystra and Iconium** [eye-KOH-nih-uhm]. Paul's two visits were about two years apart. During that time young Timothy had shown enough spiritual maturity that he was **well reported of by the brethren.** The fact that this young man had come to the attention of the older members of the church in his hometown and in a church in another town shows that he must have been spiritually mature.

Shortly before Paul embarked on this second missionary journey, he and Barnabas had a strong difference of opinion about taking John Mark as a helper on the second journey. Paul had opposed doing so because Mark had left them during the first journey (Acts 13:5,13). Therefore, Barnabas and Mark formed one missionary team, and Paul and Silas another (15:36-41). Paul thus was probably looking for someone to fulfill the kind of duties that John Mark was to do. As Timothy matured, Paul entrusted to him responsibilities of great importance.

Paul realized that Timothy was considered Jewish by Jews. A child of a mixed marriage was considered Jewish if the mother was Jewish. However, for some reason, probably his father's opposition, Timothy had not been circumcised as an infant. Thus Paul **took and circumcised him.** Paul has been criticized for doing this, because he had doggedly refused to circumcise Gentile converts, such as Titus (Gal. 2:3). Paul had a missionary purpose for circumcising Timothy. "To have had a member of his entourage be of Jewish lineage and yet uncircumcised would have hampered his effectiveness among the Jews. It was at the very least a matter of missionary strategy to circumcise Timothy (1 Cor. 9:20)."[1]

Whether to circumcise Gentile believers was the issue that led to the Jerusalem Council described in Acts 15:1-35. One of the purposes of Paul's visit was to deliver **the decrees** of **the apostles and elders** from that conference, which affirmed Paul and Barnabas for not circumcising Gentile believers. Timothy's situation, however, was different because other Jews considered him to be a Jew. Therefore, to head off any unnecessary opposition to Timothy and his work, Paul had him circumcised.

The events of verses 1-4 resulted in spiritual and numerical growth of the **churches** in that area.

Many of us grew up in Christian homes, which laid the foundation for Christian faith. For many of us it was the strength of our mothers' faith that influenced us the most. Most of us were also strongly influenced by one of more teachers or mentors who led us to walk in the way of the Lord.

A Heritage of Faith (2 Tim. 1:5-6)

*What is **unfeigned faith**? In what sense was the faith of Lois and Eunice **first**? How do people make their parents' faith their own? Why* did Paul urge Timothy to **stir up the gift**? Was Timothy more timid than most of Paul's coworkers? In what sense did Paul lay hands on Timothy?

2 Timothy 1:5: When I call to remembrance the unfeigned faith that is in thee, which dwelt first in thy grandmother Lois, and thy mother Eunice; and I am persuaded that in thee also.

This was Paul's final letter. He expected soon to be put to death. The time probably was during Nero's persecution of Christians in Rome in the middle 60s of the first century. Second Timothy is the most personal of Paul's Pastoral Letters. Paul wanted Timothy to come to Rome as soon as possible. Meanwhile, Paul wrote what could be his final words to Timothy. We don't know whether Timothy arrived in Rome before Paul's death.

As Paul faced the end of his earthly life, he was remembering people and things from the past. Thus he remembered Timothy's **unfeigned faith. Unfeigned** is *anupokriton,* which means "unhypocritical," "sincere," (NIV) or "genuine" (NKJV). Paul may have been contrasting Timothy's faith with the insincere faith of the false teachers or of former coworkers such as Demas (see 4:10).

Paul noted that this **faith . . . dwelt first in** Timothy's **grandmother Lois** and then in his **mother Eunice.** This gives some additional information to what is found in Acts 16:1-5. We learn the name of Timothy's mother, and we learn that his grandmother was also a believer. The word **first** needs to be clarified. In what sense was the faith of Lois and Eunice **first** in time before Timothy's faith? One view is that Paul was referring to their faith in God as Jews, not to their Christian faith. Others insist that it must refer to their faith in Jesus Christ.

We learn from 3:14 that one of Lois's and Eunice's ways of teaching Timothy the faith was by teaching him the Scriptures. The emphasis in 1:5 is on their faith being real and being shared with Timothy. Verse 5 also emphasizes that Timothy appropriated their faith as his own. Paul stated that he was **persuaded** ("sure," NASB, NRSV; "confident," NEB) that this **unfeigned faith** that was in Timothy's grandmother and mother was **in thee also** ("now lives in you also," NIV).

Faith is not transmitted biologically; it must be personally appropriated. Timothy grew up in a home with a believing mother and grandmother and a father who was a Greek. There likely was some conflict in the family over Eunice's faith as it pertained to Timothy. Like many women she had to be the one who taught faith to her child because her husband did not share her faith.

Timothy had made his own decision to follow Christ. The influence of Lois and Eunice was such that he followed them in their faith. We know little about Lois, but her example can encourage grandparents to have a part in sharing their faith.

2 Timothy 1:6: Wherefore I put thee in remembrance that thou stir up the gift of God, which is in thee by the putting on of my hands.

Paul reminded Timothy to **stir up the gift of God. Stir up** translates *anazopurein*, which "describes the act of rekindling the embers of a dying fire. The command does not imply that Timothy had let his spiritual flame go out. It is an appeal for a continual, vigorous use of his spiritual gifts."[2]

Some Bible students see this verse, 1 Timothy 4:12, and 2 Timothy 1:7-8 as indicators that Timothy was especially timid. This reading of these verses, however, fails to look at the big picture of Timothy's loyal and often courageous service. Unlike John Mark, Timothy stayed with the missionary team. Paul wrote often of Timothy's total dedication (see Phil. 2:20-22), and he sent him on many dangerous missions. As we read passages such as 1 Timothy 1:6-8, we should remember that Paul thought of Timothy as a son and that Paul knew this likely would be his last opportunity to encourage his younger coworker.

Another reality is the fact that each believer needs to constantly stir up the embers of his or her relation to and calling from the Lord. Faith by its very nature must be continually renewed or it will grow stale and cold. "Just because people are encouraged by someone does not mean that they are failing. It can mean that they are being encouraged to continue despite the pressure."[3]

What **gift** did Paul have in mind? He was thinking of the gift of God that enabled Timothy to serve the Lord. In Ephesians 4:11 Paul referred to church leaders as gifted people whom the Lord gave as gifts to the churches. Timothy was a gifted person, as Paul recognized when he invited him to join his missionary team.

Paul said that **the gift of God** was **in** Timothy **by the putting on** ("laying on," NIV, NKJV) **of** Paul's **hands.** Paul used similar words in 1 Timothy 4:14, which speaks of the laying on of the hands of elders. Timothy may have had hands laid on him on two different occasions, but it more likely was done at one time. When Barnabas and Saul were sent out as missionaries by the Antioch church, hands were laid on them (Acts 13:3). This signified setting apart someone for a God-called mission or ministry. It is a sign of prayer on behalf of the one being set apart. Thus Paul was reminding Timothy of his calling from God and of the prayers of others for him.

A Knowledge of the Scriptures (2 Tim. 3:14-17)

*What **scriptures** did Paul have in mind? Who taught Timothy the Scriptures? How young was he when the teaching began? In what sense are the Scriptures inspired? What are the uses of the Scriptures?*

2 Timothy 3:14-15: But continue thou in the things which thou hast learned and hast been assured of, knowing of whom thou hast learned them; ¹⁵and that from a child thou hast known the holy scriptures, which are able to make thee wise unto salvation through faith which is in Christ Jesus.

Paul reminded Timothy of what he knew of Paul's life and ministry in 3:10-13 and contrasted his life with the lives of evil, false teachers. Then he addressed Timothy in personal terms. He used the emphatic word for **thou.** Paul urged Timothy to **continue . . . in the things** that he had **learned** and **been assured of.** Paul also reminded Timothy to remember from **whom** he had **learned them.** Paul, of course, was one of Timothy's teachers, but Timothy's mother and grandmother also must have been in Paul's mind. Paul wrote of Timothy having learned the Scriptures **from a child. Child** is *brephous,* which means "an infant." Therefore, Timothy was taught the **holy scriptures** ("sacred writings," NASB, NRSV) from the time he was very young. The early years are the years of most intense learning. Children are open to be taught in those years.

The teachings Timothy received from the Scriptures made him **wise unto salvation through faith which is in Christ Jesus.** The Bible has two main purposes. The first purpose is to lead people to trust Jesus as their Lord and Savior. The Scriptures that Timothy learned at home set the stage for his conversion.

The second main purpose of the Scriptures is to help believers in their beliefs and behavior. What **scriptures** were taught to Timothy?

2 Timothy 3:16-17: All scripture is given by inspiration of God, and is profitable for doctrine, for reproof, for correction, for instruction in righteousness: ¹⁷that the man of God may be perfect, thoroughly furnished unto all good works.

The Old Testament was the Bible of the early Christians. The New Testament was in the process of being written. First-century believers looked to the Old Testament as interpreted in light of Jesus' teachings, His life, His death, and His resurrection.

Inspiration is literally "God-breathed" (NIV). Sometimes people speak of great works of literature as "inspired." In a sense, they are; however, only the Bible is inspired in the sense that it is the Word of God. Concerning Paul's statement **all scripture is given by inspiration of God, and is profitable,** Donald Guthrie wrote: "Timothy is not therefore being informed of the inspiration of Scripture, for this was a doctrine commonly admitted by Jews, but he is being reminded that the basis of its profitableness lies in its inspired character."[4]

The Word of God is the basis for what we believe and how we behave. It is useful **for doctrine** ("teaching," NIV), **for reproof** ("rebuking," NIV), **for correction** ("correcting," NIV), **for instruction** ("training," NIV) **in righteousness.** The end result of this kind of diligent use of the Bible is **that the man of God may be perfect, thoroughly furnished** ("equipped," NIV) **unto all good works.** Thus the Bible is unique not only in what it is but also in what it achieves. Those who live in the Word and by the Word find that it shapes everything about them—their values, their attitudes, their ambitions, their actions. We never graduate from studying and following the Word of God. The Word speaks to small children, and it speaks to us at each stage of life. We see new things in familiar passages as we experience new things in life.

A Responsibility to Teach Others (2 Tim. 4:1-5)

*What did Paul tell Timothy to do? How did Paul emphasize his responsibility? What is meant by **in season** and **out of season**? What did Paul mean by **itching ears**?*

2 Timothy 4:1-5: I charge thee therefore before God, and the Lord Jesus Christ, who shall judge the quick and the dead at his appearing and his kingdom; [2]Preach the word; be instant in season, out of season; reprove, rebuke, exhort with all long-suffering and doctrine. [3]For the time will come when they will not endure sound doctrine; but after their own lusts shall they heap to themselves teachers, having itching ears; [4]and they shall turn away their ears from the truth, and shall be turned unto fables. [5]But watch thou in all things, endure afflictions, do the work of an evangelist, make full proof of thy ministry.

These verses emphasizes the responsibility of Timothy in turn to preach and teach the Bible to others.

Verse 1 shows the basis for Paul's final **charge** to Timothy. Paul was facing death. Thus he was thinking much about standing before the Lord. He reminded Timothy that we live and shall stand some day **before God, and the Lord Jesus Christ.** The Lord **shall judge the quick** ("living," NIV) **and the dead at his appearing.** Paul expressed his own confidence in familiar passages (see 2 Tim. 1:12; 4:6-8). His assurance was based on the grace of God that had saved him and guided him to serve the Lord. Now he was about to pass the torch to Timothy and other younger believers.

The basic exhortation among many was **preach the word.** The other exhortations in verse 2 seem to be subpoints under this task. **Be instant in season, out of season** could refer to Timothy's own changing moods and circumstances or it could refer to times when others listen and when they reject the message. Both would happen in Timothy's life. He needed to continue to preach the word no matter how he felt or how people responded. A preacher must comfort the afflicted and afflict the comfortable. The negative side of Timothy's ministry is seen in the words **reprove** and **rebuke.** The more positive side of preaching is in the word **exhort.** This is *parakaleson,* which can also can mean "encourage" (NIV).

Verses 3-4 predict hard times ahead for preachers of the Word of God. Paul stated, **The time will come when** some people **will not endure sound doctrine.** Instead, they will **heap to themselves teachers, having** ("because they have," NKJV) **itching ears.** Who had the **itching ears** and what does that expression mean? The hearers had the itching ears. "They will gather around them a great number of teachers to say what their itching ears want to hear" (NIV). Further, **they shall turn away their ears from the truth, and shall be turned unto fables** ("myths," NIV). **Itching ears** is a graphic way of saying that they will listen only to what they want to hear. Every preacher knows what this means. Some people are content to allow the preacher to speak about issues that do not bring them into judgment, but they resist any preaching that focuses on their own kind of sins.

Verse 5, like verse 2, is a string of short exhortations. **Watch** may carry the idea of being prepared for whatever comes. **Endure afflictions** can apply to general troubles that come to all people, but it probably refers here to the responses of people who reject the word of truth. **Do the work of an evangelist** is crucial for anyone who preaches, teaches, or lives by the Word of God. The first purpose of the Bible is to tell the good news and invite people to turn to the Savior. **Make full proof of thy ministry** means "discharge all the duties of your ministry" (NIV).

❖ Spiritual Transformations

Timothy became a Christian and grew so much spiritually as a young man that Paul invited him to join his missionary team. Timothy had been influenced in the faith by his grandmother Lois and his mother Eunice. He had learned the Scriptures as a child, and these made him ready to find salvation. Paul wrote that the Scriptures were God-breathed and were useful in teaching right beliefs and right living. Paul exhorted Timothy to continue to preach the Word under all circumstances.

God's Word is the family's source of instruction and guidance for what we should believe and how we should behave. The Word of God is meaningful at every stage of life. Even small children need to be taught its stories and its message. The parents of these children have the primary responsibility to be their teachers.

What kind of Bible teaching did you receive as a child both at home and at church? _____

What role does the Bible play in your family now? _____

What role do you believe parents should have in teaching their children truths from the Bible? _____

What role do you have in teaching your family God's Word? _____
_____

What applications do these verses have for you at this stage in your life? _____

Prayer of Commitment: Lord, help me to apply Your Word to my life and to teach it to my children and grandchildren.

---

[1] John B. Polhill, "Acts," in *The New American Commentary*, vol. 29 [Nashville: Broadman Press, 1992], 343.

[2] Thomas D. Lea, "1,2 Timothy," in *The New American Commentary*, vol. 34 [Nashville: Broadman Press, 1992], 187-188.

[3] William D. Mounce, *Pastoral Epistles*, in the Word Biblical Commentary, vol. 46 [Nashville: Thomas Nelson Publishers, 2000], 476.

[4] Donald Guthrie, *The Pastoral Epistles*, revised edition, in the Tyndale New Testament Commentaries [Grand Rapids: William B. Eerdmans Publishing Company, 1990], 175.

The Church: The Family's Partner

Background Passage: Titus 1:5–2:15
Focal Passage: Titus 1:5,9; 2:1-8,11-15
Key Verses: Titus 2:11-12

❖ *Significance of the Lesson*

• The *Theme* of this lesson is that the church helps family members learn about God and serve Him together.

• The *Life Question* this lesson seeks to address is, Why should my family be involved actively in church?

• The *Biblical Truth* is that the church is to support and expand the family's teachings about God and His guidelines for living and is to help family members serve God.

• The *Life Impact* is to help you be involved in your church's educational ministries so your family can learn more about God and serve Him better.

Views About the Church

In a secular worldview, the church holds no place of importance. At best, it is a benevolent if somewhat misguided and antiquated organization. However, it can be used to further a person's selfish ambitions and purposes—such as aspirations to political office. Even some Christians view the church as a good organization that is on the periphery of their activities, so their participation is minimal—token and sporadic.

The biblical worldview emphasizes that the church is a vital partner in the family's work of teaching biblical truths for living. Consistent participation in the church's educational ministries is indispensable in the family's teaching task.

Who Was Titus?

Titus was a Gentile convert, perhaps led to Christ by Paul himself, who called him "my true son in our common faith" (Titus 1:4, NIV). Because

Titus was a Gentile believer, Paul resisted pressure to have him circumcised (Gal. 2:1,3). When Paul was under fire in Corinth, he sent Titus to seek to bring about reconciliation (2 Cor. 2:13; 7:6-7,13,15). Titus volunteered for another tough task—leading the Corinthians to complete their part in the offering from the Gentile churches to Jewish believers in Jerusalem (8:6,16-17,23). The Letter to Titus reflects another difficult assignment—this time in Crete (Titus 1:5,10-11; 2:15; 3:14). Paul asked Titus to meet him in Nicopolis (3:12). Shortly before Paul's death, Titus was in Dalmatia, no doubt on another assignment (2 Tim. 4:10).

Word Study: *Peculiar*

Periousion is translated "peculiar" in Titus 2:14. In our day, *peculiar* often describes people who do strange things. The meaning of the Greek word, however, is "chosen" or "special." *Periousion* is found in the Greek Old Testament to translate "peculiar" in Exodus 19:5. The emphasis is that the people belong to God in a special way. Thus many contemporary English versions translate it "special" (NKJV) or "his very own" (NIV).

❖ *Search the Scriptures*

Paul told Titus to complete what was left unfinished and to appoint elders in the churches. As Titus did this, he needed to deliver the trustworthy message of sound doctrine and consistent Christian living. Paul told Titus what to teach older men and women, who in turn were to help teach the younger generation. When Paul mentioned young men, he included Titus and the role he was to fulfill. Paul set forth the basic message of the Christian gospel and emphasized the changed lives that should result from believing the good news.

Encouragement by Church Leaders (Titus 1:5,9)

*Why did Paul leave Titus in Crete? What was his authority to appoint elders? What did Paul tell Titus to do about the **word** and **doctrine**?*
1:5,9: For this cause left I thee in Crete, that thou shouldest set in order the things that are wanting, and ordain elders in every city, as I had appointed thee. . . . ⁹Holding fast the faithful word as he hath been taught, that he may be able by sound doctrine both to exhort and to convince the gainsayers.

Paul said that he **left** Titus **in Crete.** This implies that Paul had been there for a time. If so, this would be the only biblical mention of Paul's working in Crete, a large island in the Mediterranean Sea. The only other time we know that Paul was in Crete was during the ill-fated voyage to Rome. Acts 27:12 tells us that the ship stopped there briefly. Acts 2:11 lists people from Crete being among those who heard Peter preach on Pentecost. If they believed, they may have initiated Christian work in Crete.

Paul referred to one Cretian who described the people of Crete as "liars, evil brutes, lazy gluttons" (Titus 1:12, NIV). The churches were being subjected to false teachers, against whom Paul warned Titus (1:10-16). These facts give us insight into the difficult mission entrusted by Paul to Titus.

Paul's first exhortation to Titus was to **set in order the things that are wanting** ("straighten out what was left unfinished," NIV). **Set in order** translates *epidiorthose.* This is the only time the word appears in the New Testament. It means "to set right" or "to correct." **That are wanting** ("lacking," NKJV) translates *ta leiponta,* which means "the remaining things." Paul mentioned some of the things that still needed to be done in Crete as he wrote the letter.

One important task was to **ordain** ("appoint," NIV, NKJV) **elders in every city. Elders** is one of several titles for church leaders. "Bishop" (1:7) or "overseer" (NIV) is another title for the same office. Many Bible students believe that both are the same office as pastor (see 1 Pet. 5: 1-4; Acts 20:28). What exactly was Titus's authority for appointing the elders? Some claim he was acting as a bishop, who in some denominations appoints pastors. More likely he was acting under Paul's apostolic authority. Nevertheless, "it is unlikely that Titus made such appointments without the advice and consent of the local Cretan congregation."[1]

The qualifications for **elders** are in verses 6-9. Compare these with the list in 1 Timothy 3:1-7. Verse 9 emphasizes some of the duties of an elder or other church leader. **Holding fast the faithful word as he hath been taught** is crucial for all church leaders in any century. **Sound doctrine** is emphasized in the Pastoral Letters. **Sound** is *hugiainouse,* which means "healthy." The same phrase is found again in 2:1. This stronghold on the truth was needed to deal with false teachers whose teachings were not sound and healthy but false and destructive. The elders were to hold to sound doctrine in order **to exhort and to convince the gainsayers** ("convict those who contradict," NKJV; "refute those who oppose it," NIV).

One of the destructive results of the work of the false teachers was that they subverted "whole houses" (1:11; "whole households," NKJV; "whole families," NASB). By contrast, the right kind of church leaders is a blessing to families.

When a church is what it should be, the church is an ally of Christian parents in the spiritual development of them and their children. The pastor of a church and other church leaders have the strongest influence; their teachings and example should minister to every member of the family. After all, a church is a family of faith. For many children and youth, the most influential people are their Sunday School teachers. They are often the unsung heroes of the church. Some people have taught the same age group of children or youth for many years. They teach more than one generation of children or youth.

Influence of Older Adults (Titus 2:1-5)

What qualities did Paul call for among older men? What qualities did he call for in older women? How and what were they to teach younger women? What does this teach about the Christian family?

2:1-5: But speak thou the things which become sound doctrine: ²that the aged men be sober, grave, temperate, sound in faith, in charity, in patience. ³The aged women likewise, that they be in behavior as becometh holiness, not false accusers, not given to much wine, teachers of good things; ⁴that they may teach the young women to be sober, to love their husbands, to love their children, ⁵to be discreet, chaste, keepers at home, good, obedient to their own husbands, that the word of God be not blasphemed.

Verse 1 is addressed to Titus. Paul urged him to do **things which become sound doctrine. Become** here means "in accord with" (NIV) or "are proper for" (NKJV). Such teaching was needed to refute the false teachings. The word translated **sound** is the same one used in 1:9. Titus was to provide an example of **sound doctrine** so the believers on Crete could withstand those who taught false doctrine.

Verses 2-6 summarize qualities needed for four groups in the churches: older men (v. 2), older women (v. 3), younger women (vv. 4-5), and younger men (v. 6). Paul instructed Titus in what should be expected from each group.

Aged men in this passage refers not to elders as officers in the church but to men who were considered older. Paul taught that this group should **be sober** ("temperate," NIV). They also were to be **grave,** but this doesn't mean "morose" or "gloomy." The Greek word is *semnous,* which means "reverent" (NKJV), "worthy of respect" (NIV), "serious" (NRSV), or "dignified" (NASB). **Temperate** translates *sophronas.* This word or one of its cognate words is found in the qualities of all four age groups (vv. 4,5,6). It means "self-controlled" (NIV), "prudent" (NRSV), or "sensible." (NASB). Pagan moralists often mentioned these three qualities, but the others are distinctively Christian. They were to be **sound in faith, in charity, in patience. Sound** is the same word used in 1:9 and 2:1 for sound doctrine. The word refers to what is healthy. The older men were not only to hold to *sound doctrine* but also to practice *sound behavior.* Three areas of healthy living are mentioned. **Faith** can refer to one's beliefs, but it also can refer to personal trust. **Charity** is *agape,* the kind of distinctly Christian love. **Patience** is *hupomone,* which refers to "endurance" (NIV) or "perseverance" (NASB). It is bearing up under a heavy load.

Aged women today might prefer "older" to "aged." So might their male counterparts. Paul did not here define what age. However, in listing qualifications for a widow to be placed on the church's list of widows, he restricted the list to widows who were 60 and above (1 Tim. 5:9). Paul mentioned two positive and two negative qualities for older women. On the negative side, he called on these women **not** to be **false accusers** ("slanderers, NIV, "malicious gossips," NASB). The Greek word is *diabolous,* which usually is translated "devil." He was the ultimate slanderer, and gossips are doing the devil's work as surely as people who commit sins considered to be much more serious.

Older women were also **not** to be **given to much wine.** Alcohol was a problem during the time of Paul and Titus. **Given** translates *dedoulomenas,* which means "enslaved to" or "addicted to" (NIV). Similar warnings were given to church leaders (see 1 Tim. 3:3,8; Titus 1:7).

Positively, the behavior of older women should include **holiness** ("be reverent in the way they live," NIV). They also were to be **teachers of good things.** This is one word in Greek. The compound word includes words for "good" and "teacher." Some Bible students think that Paul coined this word, *kalodidaskalous.* A specific application is their duty to **teach the young women. Teach** is the verb *sophronizosin,* which usually means to "bring someone to his senses." Here it probably has the force of "encourage" (NASB) or "admonish" (NKJV). Who were they to encourage? **The young women** of the church were to be their pupils.

This kind of teaching at times may have included a formal teaching session, but more often it was the kind of informal teaching that all believers do for one another (see Col. 3:16).

The content of what the older women taught the younger women shows us what was expected of the young group in the church. Most of these qualities were for the home. **The young women** were **to love their husbands, to love their children.** They were also **to be discreet. Discreet** ("self-controlled," NIV, NRSV; "sensible," NASB) is *sophronas,* the same word used for all four groups. They also were to be **chaste,** which means faithful to their husbands. **Keepers at home** is another compound word, *oikourgous,* which can mean "busy at home" (NIV), "homemakers" (NKJV), "managers of the household, (NRSV). **Good** ("kind," NIV) is another quality of Christian young women. Last but not least in the list is the call for married young women "to be subject to their husbands" (NIV). Paul warned the young women to do these things so **that the word of God be not blasphemed.** This warning applies to all the age groups. Failing to behave as Christians encourages unbelievers to blaspheme God.

Notice how many of these have to do with the family duties of a young woman. They are to be homemakers who love their children and their husbands, and who voluntarily submit themselves to their own husbands. The Southern Baptist Convention in 1998 adopted an addition to *The Baptist Faith and Message,* the denomination's confession of faith. One of the paragraphs deals with this issue: "The husband and wife are of equal worth before God, since both are created in God's image. The marriage relationship models the way God relates to His people. A husband is to love his wife as Christ loved the church. He has the God-given responsibility to provide for, to protect, and to lead his family. A wife is to submit herself graciously to the servant leadership of her husband even as the church willingly submits to the headship of Christ. She, being in the image of God as is her husband and thus equal to him, has the God-given responsibility to respect her husband and to serve as his helper in managing the household and nurturing the next generation."[2]

In recent decades the role of homemaker has been held up to public ridicule. Some women, when asked what they do, answer apologetically, "I'm just a housewife." Yet what calling could be higher in the eyes of God than to be a wife and mother?

Titus 2:1-5 emphasizes the need for older members of the church to teach the younger ones. Our church is a young adult-youth-children-preschool congregation. We have only a few older members by comparison. Those of us who are older are given many opportunities to influence the younger members—some by formal teaching. From time to time an older class will meet for Bible study with a class of young adults, but most of the teaching is by example and in conversations. My wife and I are among the older members. A number of younger women in our church have told her they want to be like her when they are her age.

Impact of Exemplary Teachers (Titus 2:6-8)

What was expected of young men in the church? What was expected of Titus? Why is a good example necessary for effective teaching?
2:6-8: Young men likewise exhort to be sober minded. [7]In all things showing thyself a pattern of good works: in doctrine showing uncorruptness, gravity, sincerity, [8]sound speech, that cannot be condemned; that he that is of the contrary part may be ashamed, having no evil thing to say of you.

Paul mentioned only one thing for **young men. Sober minded** ("self-controlled," NIV, NRSV; "sensible," NASB) is *sophronein*. Mentioning this group reminded Paul that Titus was of this group. Therefore, Paul spoke directly to Titus about his responsibilities as a young man and a Christian leader.

In all things he was to show himself to be **a pattern** ("an example," NIV) **of good works.** "The order is significant; example comes before precept, but the precept which accompanies it must be of the noblest kind."[3]

In doctrine he was to show **uncorruptness** ("integrity," NKJV, NIV), **gravity** ("reverence, NKJV; "seriousness," NIV), and **sincerity. Sound speech** is *logon hugie.* The word **sound** (*hugie*) usually is found with the word "doctrine," but there is also the need for healthy or sound speech. Such speaking **cannot be condemned.** The purpose of using such speech is so **that he that is of the contrary part** ("one who is an opponent," NKJV; "those who oppose you," NIV) **may be ashamed, having no evil thing to say of you.**

The importance of a good example cannot be overstated. People expect preachers and teachers to practice what they preach. As someone has put it, "More is caught than taught." This is true in the church family and it is true within the family. People may not understand all that a person tries to teach them, but they will learn from observing what the person does.

One of the favorite charges against churches and church people is that they are hypocrites who fail to do what is right and sometimes even do what is wrong. A pastor's influence is dependent on how he lives. The same is true of a Sunday School teacher. Of course, this is true within the home as the children see how consistent the behavior of their parents is with their professed beliefs.

Some of the learning that takes place in a church or home is the result of a plan, but some learning is not planned. Children, for example, may learn more about a church and its leaders by attending a business session or by going to a ball game in which a church team competes. Unfortunately, not all of this learning is what the church intends to teach. However, when the participants act as Christians should, their influence for good is great.

Instruction of God's Grace (Titus 2:11-15)

What is the relation between Christian beliefs and behavior? What two appearances did Paul mention in verses 11-15? What does grace teach? How does our hope of Christ's coming affect how we live now? From what does redemption set us free?

2:11-15: For the grace of God that bringeth salvation hath appeared to all men, [12]teaching us that, denying ungodliness and worldly lusts, we should live soberly, righteously, and godly, in this present world; [13]looking for that blessed hope, and the glorious appearing of the great God and our Savior Jesus Christ; [14]who gave himself for us, that he might redeem us from all iniquity, and purify unto himself a peculiar people, zealous of good works. [15]These things speak, and exhort, and rebuke with all authority. Let no man despise thee.

Titus 2:11-14 is one of the most familiar passages in the book. Christian beliefs and behavior go together. This is the theme of the passage. In these verses Paul wrote of two appearances. He began with the appearance of **the grace of God.** In verse 11 Paul used *epiphane* **(appeared)** to refer to Christ's first coming, and in verse 13 he used *epiphaneian* **(appearing)** to refer to Christ's future coming.

Grace (*charis*) was one of Paul's favorite words. **Grace** is the unmerited favor of God by which sinners are saved. Paul often emphasized that people cannot save themselves; only God's grace can. The words **to all men** may go either with **appeared** or with **salvation.** The *King James Version* and the *New International Version* take them with **appeared.** The *New American Standard Bible* (and the *New Revised Standard Version*) takes them with **salvation**: "For the grace of God has appeared, bringing salvation to all men." Neither way of translating this verse teaches universalism—the belief that in the end all people will be saved. The point is that **salvation** is for all people. How did the **grace of God** appear? Grace **appeared** in the coming, life, death, and resurrection of Jesus Christ.

The appearing of God's grace in Christ teaches us some things not to do and some things to do. We are to deny **ungodliness and worldly lusts.** Instead, **we should live soberly, righteously, and godly, in this present world.** Ungodly living is living as if there is no God; godly living is living out of a personal faith in God. **Soberly** ("self-controlled," NIV) translates *sophronos,* the same word used to describe each of the four age groups. Our age, like the **present world** of Paul's day, reflects the same sins. Living a Christian life in such a world is not easy. However, if we truly have experienced **the grace of God,** we are empowered to live a new life.

The **blessed hope** is the confident assurance that Jesus will come again. Christian hope is not wishful thinking; it is the confident hope that God will fulfill His promises. **Looking for,** *prosdechomenoi,* means "with eager anticipation." Christians base their assurance of this hope on what God did during Christ's first coming. His second coming will be **the glorious appearing of the great God and our Savior Jesus Christ.** This title is a strong statement of the deity of Jesus Christ.

The One who is coming is the same One **who gave himself for us,** a clear reference to Christ's death for us. This death was so that **he might redeem us. Redeem** is one of many words used to describe salvation. The word comes from the slave market of that day. Redemption referred to liberation of a slave by paying for the slave's release from slavery to freedom. By His death, the Lord redeemed **us from all iniquity.** Such deliverance leads to a new life of freedom, a different way of life. God's positive purpose of redemption was to **purify unto himself a peculiar people** ("a people that are his very own," NIV; "for His own possession," NASB). His redeemed people are to be **zealous of good works** ("eager to do what is good," NIV). This kind of wording was used in the Old Testament of Israel (Ex. 19:5).

Paul told Titus **these things speak.** Titus was to **exhort** ("encourage," NIV), **and rebuke with all authority.** He was not to allow anyone to **despise** or intimidate him.

The theme that holds these verses together focuses on Christian beliefs and the kind of living that goes with right beliefs. Many passages in the Bible tie together faith and works—that is, the faith that expresses itself in good works. Good works do not save us; but if our faith is genuine, our lives will show it. How do verses 11-15 relate to families? For one thing, they remind us that every member of the family needs the gospel of grace preached in the church. It also shows us that an experience of divine grace in salvation is demonstrated by how we live day by day, which includes how we live at home.

❖ *Spiritual Transformations*

Paul entrusted Titus with another difficult task when he left Titus in Crete to finish what had been started there. One task was to appoint elders who would teach sound doctrine and sound living, in contrast to the false teachers. Titus also was to teach each age group: older men, older women, younger women, and younger men to be self-controlled among other things. Titus himself was to be a good example of the things he taught. He was to preach the good news of Christ's first and second comings, and he was to emphasize that right beliefs lead to right behavior.

A basic premise of this lesson is that Christians belong to two families and that what applies to the family of faith and love is also true of the family of kin. In contrast to false teachers who disrupt family life, church leaders help families in many ways. Expectations for different age groups in the church family carry over into their family. Emphasis is given to the role of young women as homemakers and to the teaching of young people by older people. Leaders in churches and in homes teach as much by example as by precept. Just as sound beliefs transform the lives of church families, so do they for believers in their own families.

What verses in this lesson speak to your life at home? _____

How can you make your family life better by regular participation in church? _____

Prayer of Commitment: Lord, be the Lord of my family at home and at church.

[1]Hayne P. Griffin, "Titus," in *The New American Commentary*, vol. 34 [Nashville: Broadman Press, 1992], 278.

[2]*The Baptist Faith and Message*, Article XVIII, "The Family" [Nashville: LifeWay Christian Resources, 2000], 21.

[3]Donald Guthrie, *The Pastoral Epistles*, 207.

The Good News: The Family's Message

Background Passage: Acts 10:1-48
Focal Passage: Acts 10:1-5,23b-24,33-36,39-43
Key Verse: Acts 10:43

❖ *Significance of the Lesson*

• The *Theme* of this lesson is that families can help others know about Jesus.

• The *Life Question* addressed in this lesson is, How can my family impact others for Christ?

• The *Biblical Truth* is that Christian families are to seek opportunities to share with others the good news of salvation in Christ.

• The *Life Impact* is to help you and your family share the good news of Christ with others.

Families Sharing the Good News of Christ

In the secular worldview, Jesus is a mythical figure or at best one of history's greatest teachers. His resurrection, living presence, and ability to forgive sin are viewed as false, misguided claims. Some families profess to believe in Christ, but they live as if they did not believe in Him.

The biblical worldview asserts that Jesus came as God incarnate, lived a sinless life, died on the cross for our sins in sacrificial self-giving, arose from the grave, and lives forever. This is the good news of saving grace that is available to all people. The task of the church, of families, and of individual believers is to share this good news with all people.

The Importance of Acts 10:1–11:18

The Book of Acts tells how the good news was preached first to the Jewish people in and around Jerusalem. The apostles did a good job of this, as seen in Acts 1–5. However, they failed to take the initiative in witnessing to non-Jews. Stephen seems to have recognized the need for a world mission. After his death, many of the believers were scattered. Wherever they went, they told the good news. Philip, one of the seven chosen in Acts 6, went to Samaria and to the Ethiopian (Acts 8). Other unnamed Jewish believers went to Antioch and preached to Gentiles as well as Jews (11:19-30). Acts 10:1–11:18 is the account of how God led Simon Peter to tell the good news to Cornelius and his friends and relatives. The importance of this event is seen in the fact that this story is told twice and is the longest narrative in the Book of Acts.

Word Study: *House*

The word **house** is found a number of times in Acts 10:1–11:18. Two related Greek words are used: *oikos* and *oikia*. Most of the time these words refer to a building, but occasionally they refer to the people who reside in the house. Acts 10:2 and 11:14 use **house** to refer to the people in the building, but the other references refer to a building (10:6,17,22,30,32; 11:11,12,13).

Word Study: *Preaching*

Euangelizo means to tell or announce good news. In secular Greek culture this word was an everyday word used of any kind of good news. In the New Testament it usually refers to telling, preaching, or announcing the good news of Jesus Christ. We get our word *evangelize* from it.

❖ *Search the Scriptures*

Cornelius, a Roman centurion, and his family believed in the God of the Jews. An angel told him to send for Peter. When Peter was led by the Lord to Cornelius, the Roman had gathered together his relatives and close friends. When Peter preached the good news to them, they believed.

Seeking God as a Family (Acts 10:1-5)

What is a **centurion**? *What actions show the religious life of Cornelius? Were "God-fearing" Gentiles a distinctive group? What is the meaning of* **house**? *How did Jews view Cornelius and his family? How did Jewish Christians view him? What did the Lord tell Cornelius to do? These questions are addressed in the comments on these verses.*

Verses 1-2: **There was a certain man in Caesarea called Cornelius, a centurion of the band called the Italian band, ²a devout man, and one that feared God with all his house, which gave much alms to the people, and prayed to God always.**

Cornelius was a common name among Romans. A man named P. Cornelius Sulla had freed 10,000 slaves in 82 B.C. Many of these slaves joined the army; therefore, military people were often named **Cornelius.** The Cornelius of Acts 10 was **a centurion.** The Greek word used here is *hekatontarches.* This word for **centurion** comes from the word for "one hundred." *Kenturion* is another word for the same rank (see Mark 15:39). A Roman centurion was an officer who was responsible for 100 soldiers. Cornelius was in **the band called the Italian band. Band** translates *speires,* which was a unit in the Roman army called a "cohort" (NASB; "regiment," NKJV, NIV). One hundred men made up a century, two centuries made a maniple, three maniples made a cohort, ten cohorts made a legion of 6,000 troops. Thus a centurion led the basic unit of a legion. They were considered the backbone of the Roman army.

Caesarea refers to the city on the coast, not to Caesarea Philippi far inland. The city had been rebuilt by Herod the Great, and from A.D. 6 (when Archelaus was removed as king) Caesarea was the seat of Roman government. This was where the procurators had their main offices. The city had many Romans in it, and a large number of them were in the military. Many retired military personnel settled there.

Cornelius is the most famous of the centurions in the Bible. He was **a devout man. Devout** translates *eusebes,* which refers to a person who takes God seriously and reverently. He was **one that feared God.** Cornelius was a Gentile, but he feared the God of the Jews and sought to live by Judaism's moral teachings. **Feared** is used of Cornelius also in verses 22 and 35. It is also used of Gentiles who were in the synagogue in Antioch of Pisidia (13:16,26). According to the original language of the New Testament, this same group seems at times to be called "God-worshipers" (13:50; 16:14; 17:4,17; 18:7).

God-fearer may have been a technical term for Gentiles who worshiped the God of Israel, or it may have been simply the best way to describe Gentiles who feared and worshiped God and who kept the Jewish moral laws. In either case, there were a number of Gentiles who fit this general pattern. Cornelius had not been circumcised nor did he keep all the ceremonial laws of the Jews, which he would have been required to do if he had been a proselyte who had officially become involved in Judaism. In his travels Paul encountered many people like Cornelius. They often were more responsive to the gospel than those fully committed to Judaism. They formed the nucleus of a Christian church in many places where Paul preached. They were seekers of God who responded to the good news that Jesus was the Jewish Messiah and the Savior of the world.

Cornelius practiced two of the central marks of Judaism. He **gave much alms to the people, and prayed to God always.** "He gave generously to those in need and prayed to God regularly" (NIV). Matthew 6:1-18 shows that almsgiving and prayer were two of the main Jewish acts of righteousness. The third was fasting. Acts 10:22 says Cornelius was "a righteous and God-fearing man, who is respected by all the Jewish people" (NIV).

The most important words in verses 1-2 for this lesson on family are the words **with all his house. House** is used here to refer to his family and his servants. Since Cornelius was the husband, father, and master of his household, he was no doubt the one who had influenced his family and servants to fear God. He was the key person in leading his family to seek God.

Verses 3-5: **He saw in a vision evidently about the ninth hour of the day an angel of God coming in to him, and saying unto him, Cornelius. ⁴And when he looked on him, he was afraid, and said, What is it, Lord? And he said unto him, Thy prayers and thine alms are come up for a memorial before God. ⁵And now send men to Joppa, and call for one Simon, whose surname is Peter.**

Following this impressive introduction to Cornelius is the beginning of the action that is recorded in Acts 10:1–11:18. **About the ninth hour of the day** would be "about three in the afternoon" (NIV). Since this coincided with one of the daily prayer times in the temple, Cornelius was probably praying when he **saw . . . a vision** of **an angel of God.** The angel came to him and called him by name. Cornelius **was afraid, and said, What is it, Lord?** In the visions of Cornelius and Peter, God took the initiative in coming to them with a message. In the case of Cornelius, He sent an angel as His messenger.

The angel said, **Thy prayers and thine alms are come up for a memorial before God.** Apparently Cornelius had been praying for more light. At any rate, God had seen his generous giving and prayers as expressions of a sincere seeker of God. The angel used the language of the sacrificial system. His giving and praying had ascended to God like the sweet aroma of sacrifices. God was going to respond to this man who was so intent on knowing and serving God.

The angel told Cornelius to **send men to Joppa.** This was a city about 30 miles south of Caesarea. Cornelius was told to have the delegation ask for **Simon, whose surname is Peter.**

Reaching Friends and Relatives (Acts 10:23b-24,33)

*Whom did Cornelius send to find Simon? What had prepared Simon to receive this delegation? Whom did Simon take with him when he went to see Cornelius? How long did it take for the actions of verses 1-24? What had Cornelius been doing in the meanwhile? In what sense were all those in the house of Cornelius **present before God**?*

Verses 23b-24,33: **And on the morrow Peter went away with them, and certain brethren from Joppa accompanied him. ²⁴And the morrow after they entered into Caesarea. And Cornelius waited for them, and had called together his kinsmen and near friends. . . . ³³Immediately therefore I sent to thee; and thou hast well-done that thou art come. Now therefore are we all here present before God, to hear all things that are commanded thee of God.**

Acts 10:1–11:18 can be divided into seven scenes. Scene 1 was verses 1-8. These verses tell of Cornelius's vision and his sending of his servants and a devout soldier to Caesarea to find Simon Peter. Verses 9-16 describe Peter's vision. Peter was puzzled by this vision, in which he was told not to call anything unclean if God had declared it clean. The vision related to the unclean food laws of Judaism. As he was puzzling over this vision, the delegation from Cornelius arrived. This begins the scene in verses 17-23. The Spirit told Peter to go with the messengers. They explained why they had come by telling Peter of Cornelius and his vision. They mentioned that Cornelius was well thought of by the Jews.

The next morning they began the trip to Caesarea. Peter took with him **certain brethren from Joppa.** Peter knew that he could be called on to explain why he broke Jewish tradition by going into the home of a Gentile. Acts 11:12 shows that he took six Jewish Christian brothers with him. This proved to be a wise move because Peter was called on to explain his actions.

Cornelius had his vision on day 1. His delegation arrived in Joppa on day 2. They spent the night of day 3 on the road. They arrived in Caesarea on day 4. The fourth scene in the story is in verses 24-33.

Cornelius had not been idle during this time. He **waited for them, and had called together his kinsman and near friends** ("relatives and close friends," NIV, NKJV). This is the key verse for this lesson on a family sharing its faith with others. Cornelius wanted all his relatives and all his close friends to hear what Peter had to say.

When Peter arrived, Cornelius fell at his feet; but Peter quickly told him that he was a man. When Peter went into the house of the Gentile, he told Cornelius that he was breaking the law of his people, which forbade a Jew to have fellowship with a Gentile. However, Peter said that he was there because God had taught him not to call anyone unclean. This shows that Peter had learned the lesson of the vision he had had. At Peter's request, Cornelius explained why he had summoned Peter. Cornelius told of his own vision. Then he thanked Peter for coming and he said, **We** are **all here present before God, to hear all things that are commanded thee of God.** Cornelius realized they were acting according to God's will and the Lord was present with them.

The key words for this point in this lesson are **kinsman and near friends.** Cornelius was not yet a full-fledged Christian, but he had the heart of a missionary. He anticipated that Peter was going to declare good news, and he wanted his friends as well as his family to hear it also.

We live in a time much like the world of Simon Peter and Cornelius. The Christian family has been battered by the non-Christian culture in which we live. Charles Colson wrote, "In postmodern America, the family is being assaulted on many fronts, from books to popular magazines, on television and in movies, through state and federal policies. This systematic deconstruction of the oldest, most basic social institution is a prime cause of the social chaos in America in recent decades."[1] Colson called on Christians to understand and practice the Christian worldview. "Believers should be encouraged to treat their own families as a ministry—a mission to the surrounding culture."[2]

Cornelius was a soldier, probably a career military man. If he was like soldiers of today, he and his family moved from time to time. The first century was a mobile society. Thus believers and their families had opportunities of witnessing to many groups. This is surely true in our time. Some dedicated military families have helped start churches wherever they were assigned. Each one has opportunities, but the family as a whole also has an opportunity to influence those about them. Whether or not your family moves about, your family has opportunities to influence others for Christ.

Telling the Good News (Acts 10:34-36,39-43)

What important lesson had Peter learned? Was Cornelius saved by his goodness? What were the main points of the good news that Peter preached in the house of Cornelius? How does verse 43 sum up the proper response to the gospel?

Verses 34-36: **Then Peter opened his mouth, and said, Of a truth I perceive that God is no respecter of persons:** **[35]but in every nation he that feareth him, and worketh righteousness, is accepted with him.** **[36]The word which God sent unto the children of Israel, preaching peace by Jesus Christ: (he is Lord of all).**

Verse 34 is a key text in the Bible. It shows a most important lesson that Peter had learned. The words **opened his mouth** was a way of alerting a reader that what follows is very important (see Matt. 5:2; Acts 8:35). What did Peter mean by **no respecter of persons**? The Greek word is *prosopolemptes.* This comes from a Hebrew idiom that means "to lift a face." Lifting someone's face meant to show special favor toward that person. Thus judges were warned not to do this. That is, they were not to judge based on appearances. A rich man was not to be favored above a poor man. "God does not show favoritism" (NIV). He is impartial in His dealings with humanity. This statement was the opposite of the view that Peter had been taught all his life—that God is partial toward the children of Israel. They were His chosen people, but God's intention from the beginning was to show His grace to all people.

Verse 35 further explains this concept. Whoever fears God and lives righteously **is accepted with him.** Does this mean that they are saved by their piety and goodness? John R. W. Stott wrote, "The emphasis is that Cornelius' Gentile nationality was acceptable, so that he had no need to become a Jew, not that his own righteousness was adequate so that he had no need to become a Christian."[3] John B. Polhill said: "Cornelius, like Abraham, had shown himself to be a man of faith and trust in God. God was already working his grace in him, and it manifested itself in his good deeds. Now God would show him his greatest grace in the gospel of Jesus Christ and the gift of the Spirit."[4]

Verse 36 points to the Jewish origin of the gospel and to its universal scope. It is **the word which God sent unto the children of Israel.** It involved **preaching peace.** The One who brings that peace is **Jesus Christ: (he is the Lord of all),** not just Lord of Israel. Jesus Christ is the heart of the good news.

Verses 39-43: **And we are witnesses of all things which he did both in the land of the Jews, and in Jerusalem; whom they slew and hanged on a tree:** **⁴⁰Him God raised up the third day, and showed him openly;** **⁴¹not to all the people, but unto witnesses chosen before of God, even to us, who did eat and drink with him after he rose from the dead.** **⁴²And he commanded us to preach unto the people, and to testify that it is he which was ordained of God to be the Judge of quick and dead.** **⁴³To him give all the prophets witness, that through his name whosoever believeth in him shall receive remission of sins.**

Verses 37-38 describe the message of Jesus' life, inaugurated after the baptism of John and the anointing of the Spirit by God. Jesus "went about doing good, and healing all that were oppressed of the devil; for God was with him" (v. 38).

Peter declared, **We are witnesses of all things which he did.** As an apostle, Peter had been with Jesus and had been commissioned to bear witness to the life, death, and resurrection of Jesus. The Lord was slain when he was **hanged on a tree.** (See Gal. 3:13 for another reference to the cross as a tree.) But God did not allow the forces of darkness to prevail. **God raised** Him **up.** Not everyone saw Jesus after His resurrection, but **witnesses chosen before of God** saw Him. The certainty of the resurrection was revealed when the risen Lord ate and drank with His followers. The crucified, risen Lord **commanded** the witnesses **to preach unto the people.** They also were to declare that Jesus Christ **was ordained of God to be the Judge of quick and dead** ("the living and the dead," NIV).

The Book of Acts contains several sermons, especially sermons preached by Peter and by Paul. The heart of their messages of good news was the historical reality of Jesus Christ's death and resurrection. When Peter and Paul preached to non-Christians, they ended by calling on the hearers to turn to the Lord and be saved. Verse 43 is such an invitation. **All the prophets** bore **witness** to the Christ and declared that **through his name whosoever believeth in him shall receive remission of sins.** If Cornelius were saved already, Peter would not have issued this evangelistic invitation. Peter and those who came with him were joyfully amazed that the Gentiles believed and were filled with the Spirit (vv. 44-48). The final scene occurred when Peter was called on to explain why he went into the house of a Gentile (11:1-18). Peter showed step by step how the Lord led him, and the six witnesses confirmed what Peter said. Thus Peter learned that God wants to save Gentiles as well as Jews.

What has been the impact of each of the four lessons in this unit?

- Parents have the primary responsibility to teach their children to love God and to live by His commandments.
- The Bible is the Christian family's guidebook for beliefs and behavior.
- The church and the family are partners in their common ministries.
- Not only individuals but also families have an influence on others for Christ.

❖ *Spiritual Transformations*

Cornelius was a God-fearing Gentile whose devout life was shared by his family and servants. He was told by an angel to send for Simon Peter. When Peter got this message, he went to Cornelius's house and found that Cornelius had invited his relatives and close friends. Peter preached the good news to Cornelius and the others.

The applications of this lesson to families today are these: (1) All the members of a family need to hear the good news of Jesus Christ. (2) The family as well as the individuals in it have influence for the Lord.

What kind of witness and influence has your family had on neigh-bors and friends? _____

*What can you do to make the Christian testimony and influence of your family more effective?*_____

Prayer of Commitment: Lord, help me to do my part in leading my family to have a positive testimony for You.

[1]Charles Colson and Nancy Pearcey, *How Now Shall We Live?* [Wheaton: Tyndale House Publishers, Inc., 1999], 318.

[2]Colson, *How Now Shall We Live?* 326.

[3]John R. W. Stott, *The Spirit, the Church, and the World: The Message of Acts* [Downers Grove: InterVarsity Press, 1990], 190.

[4]Polhill, "Acts," NAC, 261.

Study Theme

Telling the Lost About Jesus

If someone you loved made a death bed request of you, you probably would do everything possible to do what was asked of you. The Lord Jesus had some final words for us. These words were spoken after He had been raised from the dead; and they were a command, not a request. He said, "You shall receive power when the Holy Spirit has come upon you; and you shall be witnesses to Me in Jerusalem, and in all Judea and Samaria, and to the end of the earth" (Acts 1:8, NKJV). This clear call to be personal witnesses and to be witnesses to the whole world combines the two closely related topics in this unit: personal witnessing and global missions.

This four-session study is designed to help Christian adults become committed to personal witnessing and global missions as a lifestyle. Studies will explore passages from the Book of Acts that focus on the fact that believers need to know and to tell the good news; that the good news is for people of all cultures; that God calls some people to go to other places to tell the good news about Jesus; and that all Christians have a duty to tell the good news about Jesus in all situations so that people will come to know and love Him.

The four lessons cover *what to tell* (the essentials of the good news about Jesus), *who to tell* (all people, including those who are culturally different from you), *where to tell* (believers go to other places to tell the peoples of the world the good news about Jesus), and *why to tell* (because people who do not know Jesus are lost in sin and without a Savior). The biblical events for these lessons are (1) Peter's sermon at Pentecost, (2) Philip's testimony to the Ethiopian, (3) Paul's first missionary journey, and (4) Paul's work in Athens.

Do you know the essentials of the good news? Would you be able to share them with someone else? _____

How do you feel about people from other cultures whom you encounter? _____

Have you ever considered a volunteer missions trip? _____

Do you really believe that people without Jesus Christ are lost in sin and doomed to hell? _____

Week of November 4

Essentials of the Good News

Background Passage: Acts 2:1-41
Focal Passage: Acts 2:14,22-24,32,36-41
Key Verse: Acts 2:38

❖ *Significance of the Lesson*

• The *Theme* of this lesson is that believers need to know and to tell the essentials of the good news.

• The *Life Question* this lesson seeks to address is, What are the essentials of the good news about Jesus that I need to tell people?

• The *Biblical Truth* is that people need to know that Jesus was crucified, that He was raised from the dead, and that He will forgive their sins and give them new life when they repent and trust Him as their Savior.

• The *Life Impact* is to help you tell the lost the essentials of the good news about Jesus.

• This is the **Evangelism Lesson** for this quarter.

Worldviews About Jesus and the Good News

Many adults do not believe the message about Jesus is what the world needs to hear. They place higher value on better education; better healthcare; better economies; better political systems; greater religious diversity, toleration, and acceptance. In fact, many adults think the message about Jesus' resurrection and continued life is fiction and falsehood. Jesus may have been a historical figure, but at the most He was a martyred teacher. Thus they consider naive those who believe in and tell the message of the death and resurrection of Jesus.

The biblical worldview emphasizes that God gave His Son, Jesus, who voluntarily gave His life on the cross for people's salvation. He was buried, but God raised Him from the dead. Jesus lives and gives forgiveness and full life to people who place their trust in Him. All Christians are to be witnesses concerning these things.

Word Study: *Repent*

Metanoeo is the Greek word for "repent" in Acts 2:38. Literally, it means to "change your mind." However, the word often is used like the Old Testament word for "repent" (*sub*) to refer to a total change of life, not merely to a change of one's mind but to a change of one's attitudes and actions. Repentance and faith go together. Sometimes they are both listed (as in 20:21). At other times, only one is mentioned; however, both are assumed. Repentance and faith are two sides of the same response to Jesus Christ. We turn from sin and turn to the Lord.

❖ *Search the Scriptures*

After the coming of the Spirit on the day of Pentecost, individual believers witnessed and Peter preached. The good news he preached focused on the life, death, and resurrection of Jesus. When the people asked what to do, Peter told them to repent and be baptized, and promised they would receive forgiveness and the Holy Spirit.

In examining how Peter announced the good news, we will see him taking the initiative, then sharing the good news, and finally calling for response.

Taking the Initiative (Acts 2:14)

How was Peter, who had denied the Lord, able to preach boldly? What was the setting for his sermon? To whom was he speaking? How did he get their attention?

Verse 14: But Peter, standing up with the eleven, lifted up his voice, and said unto them, Ye men of Judea, and all ye that dwell at Jerusalem, be this known unto you, and hearken to my words.

The believers had obeyed Jesus by waiting in Jerusalem for the coming of the Spirit. Three signs marked the coming of the Spirit: the sound of wind, the flames of fire, and the speaking in other languages (2:1-4). Jews from all over the ancient world were in Jerusalem for the feast of Pentecost. Verse 10 refers also to "proselytes." These were Gentiles who had converted to Judaism. They, along with the Jews in Judea, heard the testimonies in their own languages (vv. 5-11). Then some tried to explain away what was happening by accusing the disciples of being drunk (vv. 12-13).

At that point, **Peter** stood and spoke to the crowd. He was not alone. He was with the other **eleven** apostles (a replacement for Judas had been chosen [1:15-26]). We are impressed at the change in Simon Peter as he took the initiative to speak. Only a few weeks earlier he had denied the Lord three times. What had happened to make the difference? For one thing, Peter had seen the Lord after His resurrection and had been forgiven and recommissioned. Second, he had been filled with the Holy Spirit.

Peter's listeners are described in verses 9-11. On the special feasts of the Jews it was the custom for male Jews to gather in Jerusalem. Since many Jews lived outside of Judea, there were Jews and proselytes from all over the world.

Peter seized the opportunity presented by the coming of the Spirit, the testimony of individual believers, and the accusation of being drunk. He used words designed to challenge them to **hearken** ("listen carefully," NIV) to what he was going to say.

Peter began by denying that the believers were drunk. He explained the supernatural signs they had seen as fulfillment of the prophecy of Joel 2:28-32. The prophecy told how the Lord would pour out His Spirit and would save whoever called on the name of the Lord. Peter declared that Pentecost inaugurated the age of the Spirit.

This lesson is on personal witnessing. Peter was preaching to many people, but he did some things that also apply to one-on-one witnessing. He was sensitive to opportunities given by the Lord. He relied on the Holy Spirit. He took the initiative. He began where his listeners were, and he spoke of things of interest to them.

Sharing the Good News (Acts 2:22-24,32,36)

*What was the purpose of the miracles of Jesus? In what sense was the death of Jesus the plan and purpose of God? In what sense was it a sin for which people were guilty? How can people be held accountable for doing what was the purpose of God? How did the resurrection loosen the **pains of death**? In what sense were the apostles unique **witnesses**? In what sense are all believers witnesses? How did Peter describe the exaltation of Jesus? Whom did he accuse of the death of Jesus?*

Verses 22-24: Ye men of Israel, hear these words; Jesus of Nazareth, a man approved of God among you by miracles and wonders and signs, which God did by him in the midst of you, as ye

yourselves also know: [23]**Him, being delivered by the determinate counsel and foreknowledge of God, ye have taken, and by wicked hands have crucified and slain:** [24]**Whom God hath raised up, having loosed the pains of death: because it was not possible that he should be held of it.**

These verses are the heart of Peter's sermon and also the heart of the good news. They point to the life, death, and resurrection of Jesus. After calling on his listeners to pay attention, Peter spoke of the incarnate ministry of **Jesus of Nazareth.** Jesus was fully human and fully divine. Peter said that Jesus was **a man approved** ("accredited," NIV) **of God. Approved** translates *apodedeigmenon.* This "is a semitechnical term often found in Greek papyri and inscriptions for office holders. It can either be used of those who already hold office and for those who have received appointment but have not yet entered into active service in the office. The latter sense seems to fit the context here. Peter pictured Jesus in his earthly ministry as being designated by God as Messiah but as only entering into the active function of that role upon his death and resurrection."[1]

Jesus was shown to be more than **a man** by **miracles and wonders and signs, which God did by him in the midst of you. Miracles** translates *dunamesi,* which emphasizes the mighty power of miracles. **Wonders** translates *terasi,* which points to the sense of awe resulting from the miracles. **Signs** translates *semeiois,* which views miracles as pointing to something. The miracles that God wrought through Jesus were acts of power and compassion, which caused awe and wonder, and which pointed to who Jesus is.

In verse 23, Peter proclaimed two important aspects of the crucifixion of Jesus. From the divine perspective, Jesus was **delivered by the determinate counsel** ("set purpose," NIV) **and foreknowledge of God** (see also 4:28). The atoning death of Jesus Christ was part of God's plan from the beginning. Jesus accepted the cross as the will of His Father. In this sense, Jesus was the Lamb of God whose death was "foreordained before the foundation of the world" (1 Pet. 1:20). Looking at the cross from the human perspective, it was humanity's worst sin. Although God delivered Jesus, and Jesus offered Himself, Peter said to His hearers, **Him . . . ye have taken, and by wicked hands have crucified and slain.**

The first part of verse 23 shows that the cross was central to the eternal plan of God to provide salvation for sinners. Jesus was not a martyr who was seized and crucified without His willingness or without God being in control. Although it was God's plan, those who crucified Him were guilty of their sin. "Peter carefully balanced the elements of God's divine purposes and the human responsibility for the crucifixion of Jesus. In the paradox of divine sovereignty and human freedom, Jesus died as the result of deliberate human decision made in the exercise of their God-given freedom of choice."[2]

The crucifixion of Jesus reveals God's eternal love. It shows that there is a cross in the heart of God. At the same time, it shows human sin at its worst. Who was responsible for the crucifixion of Jesus? In this sermon, Peter accused the Jews of Jerusalem. The Jewish religious leaders were directly responsible (3:17; 13:27). But Pilate and the Roman soldiers also were involved. **By wicked hands** probably means "with the help of wicked men" (NIV). In a larger sense, all sinful humanity crucified the Lord. He died for the sins of all of us. The kinds of self-interest seen in the first-century sinners are also the sins of people today. Rome had the best system of justice in the ancient world. The Jews had the best religion. Yet the best justice system and the best religious system conspired to crucify the Son of God. The love of God and the sins of people were on a collision course; the cross was the point in history where they collided.

In verse 24 Peter proclaimed the good news of the resurrection of Jesus. **God . . . raised up** Jesus. Two things are said about this supreme biblical miracle. For one thing, God **loosed the pains of death. Pains** is the Greek word for "birth pangs." This analogy may have been intended only to communicate the depth of the pains, or it could have implied the new life that is beyond the pain. The second thing is that **it was not possible that he should be held of it** ("it was impossible for death to keep its hold on him," NIV).

The hymn writer pictured this great triumph:

> Death cannot keep his prey, Jesus, my Savior!
> He tore the bars away, Jesus, my Lord!
> Up from the grave He arose,
> With a mighty triumph o'er His foes;
> He arose a victor from the dark domain,
> And He lives forever with His saints to reign.
> He arose! He arose! Hallelujah! Christ arose![3]

Verses 32,36: **This Jesus hath God raised up, whereof we all are witnesses. . . . [36]Therefore let all the house of Israel know**

assuredly, that God hath made that same Jesus, whom ye have crucified, both Lord and Christ.

Peter supported the truth of the resurrection in two ways: First, he quoted Old Testament predictions of it. Verses 25-28 are a quotation of Psalm 16:8-11, a psalm of David in which he spoke of escaping death. Since David was dead and his body decayed in a grave, Peter concluded that David was speaking of Jesus (vv. 29-31). The second way of supporting the truth of the resurrection was to emphasize that he and the other apostles were **witnesses** that **Jesus hath God raised** ("God has raised this Jesus to life, and we are all witnesses of the fact," NIV).

Just before He ascended to heaven, Jesus said, "You will receive power when the Holy Spirit comes on you; and you will be my witnesses in Jerusalem, and in all Judea and Samaria, and to the ends of the earth" (1:8, NIV). The apostles were eyewitnesses of the risen Lord. Their testimony is the New Testament. Acts 1:8 applied especially to them, but it also is the Lord's command to every believer in every generation. Witnesses tell what they know from personal experience. Believers' witness is based on the inspired Scriptures and verified by our own experience with the Spirit of the crucified-risen Lord Jesus.

Peter spoke of the exaltation of the Lord to the right hand of God, a promise fulfilled from Psalm 110:1 (vv. 33-35). This set the stage for the climactic verse 36. Peter wanted to **let all the house of Israel know assuredly, that God hath made that same Jesus, whom ye have crucified, both Lord and Christ.** Once again there is an emphasis of the exaltation of Jesus and the guilt of the people for crucifying the Son of God. When the forces of darkness condemned and executed Jesus, they condemned Him to the death on the cross. But God reversed their condemnation and turned it back on them. The word **made** does not mean that Jesus did not become **Lord and Christ** until that time. Jesus was the Son of God from before the foundation of the world. But His death and resurrection declared His glory to all who believed. God exalted Jesus as the Lord and Messiah. Someday God will cause every knee to bow and every tongue to confess Him as Lord (Phil. 2:9-11).

The heart of the sermon by Peter stressed two events as the heart of the good news: the death of Jesus and His resurrection from the dead. Peter also emphasized two witnesses to the truth of these events: the Old Testament prophets and the witness of the apostles. Peter and Paul consistently pointed to the death and resurrection of the Lord Jesus as the content of the Christian good news (see also

1 Cor. 15:3-4). These two events go together. They are mentioned in most of the major sermons to the lost in the Book of Acts (3:14-15; 10:39-40; 13:26-30; 26:23). As we bear witness to the good news, our words ought to major on the atoning death and victorious resurrection of Jesus as the basis for forgiveness of sins and new life in the Spirit.

Calling for Response (Acts 2:37-41)

*How is the people's conviction of sin described? What is the relationship of repentance and faith? What is the relationship of repentance and faith to forgiveness of sins? What is the relationship of baptism to forgiveness of sins? What is the forgiveness of sins? What is the gift of the Holy Spirit? In what sense was the promise to their children? Who were **all that are afar off**? What is believer's baptism?*

Verses 37-38: Now when they heard this, they were pricked in their heart, and said unto Peter and to the rest of the apostles, Men and brethren, what shall we do? [38]Then Peter said unto them, Repent, and be baptized everyone of you in the name of Jesus Christ for the remission of sins, and ye shall receive the gift of the Holy Ghost.

Being confronted with their guilt in crucifying the One whom God made Lord and Christ convicted the people of their sins—**they were pricked in** ("cut to," NIV; "pierced to," NASB) **their heart.** The Holy Spirit was at work (see John 16:8-11).

They addressed a question **unto Peter and to the rest of the apostles.** The question reminds us of the question that the people asked John the Baptist, "What shall we do?" (see Luke 3:10,12,14). Addressing the apostles as **men and brethren,** they asked, **What shall we do?** This question is broader in scope than the question of the Philippian jailer, "What must I do to be saved?" (Acts 16:30). That may explain why Peter's answer was broader in scope than Paul's was to the jailer.

Repent means to turn away from sin; it assumes faith in the sense of turning to the Lord. Repentance and faith are two sides of the same coin. Sometimes one or the other is used as the response that leads to salvation; sometimes both appear together. But both are involved.

The most controversial part of this passage concerns the relationship of baptism to forgiveness of sins. Some people believe that Peter was saying that repentance and baptism result in **the remission of sins.** If this were the only verse on the subject, a case could be made for this position. However, other passages do not make baptism a condition for forgiveness and salvation. Most of the other references to forgiveness and salvation in the Book of Acts show that baptism is conditioned on repentance and faith. (3:19; 10:43; 16:31). All those who believed were baptized, but the baptism came after they had repented of sin and trusted in Jesus.

The word **for** translates *eis,* which usually means "in order for," but it also can mean "on the basis of." Matthew 12:41 says that the people of Nineveh "repented at the preaching of Jonah." "At" is the same word, *eis.* But it does not mean here that they repented "in order to receive" but "on the basis of." Thus verse 38 may be translated, "Repent, and let each of you be baptized in the name of Jesus Christ *for/on the basis of* the forgiveness of your sins."[4]

If someone asked me the broad question that Peter were asked, I probably would say something like this: "First, you need to be saved by repenting of sin and trusting Jesus as your Lord and Savior. Then you need to be baptized and to become active in the church." If I was asked the jailer's question, I would talk about repenting and believing.

This does not mean that baptism is not important—because it is. The New Testament knows virtually nothing of an unbaptized believer. Baptism is the way New Testament believers publicly declared their faith and commitment to Jesus. It was the way they entered into the fellowship of the church. It signified death and resurrection: Jesus' death and resurrection, their own spiritual death to sin and resurrection to new life, and the future resurrection (Rom. 6:3-5).

What is **remission** ("forgiveness," NIV) **of sins**? This is one of many New Testament words to describe coming into a right relationship with God. The Greek word *aphesis* is from the realm of human relations. Forgiveness means to remove a barrier to fellowship that results from one person hurting another. Just as in human relations, the forgiving person must absorb the hurt and offer reconciliation. The cross is the ultimate expression of the cost of forgiveness of sins against God.

The gift of the Holy Ghost ("Holy Spirit," NIV) is not the same as the gifts of the Spirit that are mentioned in Romans, 1 Corinthians, and Ephesians. In verse 38 the Spirit Himself is the gift. When a person becomes a Christian, the Holy Spirit comes into the person's life (Rom.8:9). The Spirit is active in convicting of sin, in regeneration, and in transforming our lives.

Some people believe that Pentecost is a formula for what happens in the lives of dedicated Christians. That is, if a believer prays earnestly enough and waits for the Spirit, the Spirit comes as a second blessing and shows His presence by enabling the person to speak in tongues. We believe that Pentecost was a once-for-all event with unique signs that signified its importance as the beginning of the age of the Spirit and of the church.

Verses 39-41: **For the promise is unto you, and to your children, and to all that are afar off, even as many as the Lord our God shall call. [40]And with many other words did he testify and exhort, saying, Save yourselves from this untoward generation. [41]Then they that gladly received his word were baptized: and the same day there were added unto them about three thousand souls.**

Your children did not mean their faith would automatically become that of their children. It meant the same good news would be available for their children and for future generations, but each person must make a personal decision. **All that are afar off** probably refers to the Gentiles, who were to receive the same good news.

Peter testified with **many other words.** This shows that his entire sermon was not recorded in verses 14-39. The gist of what he said is seen in the words, **save yourselves from this untoward** ("corrupt," NIV) **generation.** This kind of description is used in the Bible for a generation that is evil and unfaithful to God. This has been true to some degree for each generation.

They that gladly received his word were baptized. All who believed were baptized, but *only* those who believed were baptized. We believe in baptism for believers only. This rules out infant baptism and baptism designed to secure forgiveness of sins. By being baptized the people showed they were repenting and believing. They were publicly declaring they were followers of Jesus. They were identifying themselves with other believers in the church.

John Stott gave a summary of the gospel for today based on Acts 2. He identified *the gospel events* as the death and resurrection of Jesus, *the gospel witnesses* as the Old Testament and the apostles (whose testimony became the New Testament), *the gospel promises* as forgiveness of sins and the gift of the Spirit, *the gospel conditions* as repentance and faith, followed by baptism.[5] Another might be *the gospel results* as baptism and the church.

This is the first lesson in a study of missions. It has dealt with the basic expression of a missionary spirit—personal witnessing. One does not have to cross the ocean to do this; in fact, if a believer does not witness to those who are near, it is doubtful the person will witness to people anywhere. We are to tell the good news.

Christ became a man on earth,
Tell the good news, tell the good news;
Gave His life for man's rebirth,
Tell the good news, tell the good news.
Christ arose and to heaven went,
Tell the good news, tell the good news;
All may follow who repent,
Tell the good news, tell the good news.[6]

❖ *Spiritual Transformations*

After the coming of the Spirit on the day of Pentecost, Peter took the initiative in preaching to the people. He shared the good news of the life, death, and resurrection of Jesus. He called for repentance and for baptism and promised forgiveness of sins and the gift of the Spirit.

This lesson helps us see the biblical pattern for telling the good news and what we are to tell. The pattern includes the following: relying on the Spirit, beginning where people are, focusing on the death and resurrection of Jesus, sharing your own testimony based on the Bible, calling for repentance and faith, promising forgiveness and the presence of the Spirit for those who believe, and leading people to baptism and church membership.

At what points do you need to make changes to become an effective witness for Christ? _____

*To whom is the Lord leading you as a witness for Him?*_____

Prayer of Commitment: Lord, empower me by Your Spirit to be a more effective witness for You.

[1]Polhill, "Acts," NAC, 111.

[2]Polhill, "Acts," NAC, 112.

[3]Robert Lowry, "Low in the Grave He Lay," *The Baptist Hymnal* [Nashville: Convention Press, 1991], No. 160.

[4]Polhill, "Acts," NAC, 117.

[5]John Stott, *The Spirit, the Church, and the World*, 80-81.

[6]Gene Bartlett, "Tell the Good News," No. 566, *The Baptist Hymnal*, 1991.

Good News for All Cultures

Bible Passage: Acts 8:26-40
Key Verses: Acts 8:34-35

❖ *Significance of the Lesson*

• The *Theme* of this lesson is that Jesus wants His followers to tell lost people about Him regardless of their cultural differences.
• The *Life Question* addressed in this lesson is, Why should I care whether people who are culturally different from me hear about Jesus?
• The *Biblical Truth* is that believers are to tell lost people the good news about Jesus regardless of their cultural differences.
• The *Life Impact* is to help you be a witness to people who are culturally different from you.

Attitudes Toward People from Different Cultures

In the secular worldview, people care for themselves, people who are closest to them, and people who are like them. Sometimes they view people from different cultures with suspicion, indifference, and disdain. Some secular-oriented people are concerned to help people who are different, but they do not believe that the good news of Jesus is what these people need.

In the biblical worldview, God is not partial to any group but loves all people and wants them to hear the good news and be saved. He calls Christians to cross barriers to share the good news with other people, regardless of cultural differences. Some Christians struggle with showing genuine love for people who are different. Often this is based on stereotyped attitudes toward various ethnic identities and people groups. Some believers have a provincial attitude that does not see beyond a limited horizon, ignoring people within that horizon if they are different.

What Is a Missionary?

Jerry Rankin, president of the International Mission Board, said, "Missions is cross-cultural witness of sharing Jesus Christ with the lost.

I would emphasize the cross-cultural aspect, as I feel this is the only thing that distinguishes missions from evangelism—leading the lost to know Jesus Christ as Savior."[1]

Culture for many people means to be accomplished in the arts and social graces. We speak of some persons of a high socio-economic level as being "cultured" or "having culture." But missionary use of the word *culture* refers to the common characteristics of a distinctive group of people. Today, many missionaries speak not so much of "nations" but of "people groups" within nations. One nation may have within it many people groups—those who share a common history, values, traditions, customs, and so forth. R. Alton James pointed out that in 1998 there were approximately 11,874 ethno-linguistic people groups in the world. Of these, 3,915 are the least evangelized or unreached peoples.[2]

When a Christian from one cultural background or people group tells the good news to members of a separate people group, that Christian is acting as a missionary.

Word Study: *Guide*

"Guide" in Acts 8:31 is the Greek word *hodegesei.* This word can be used in a literal or in a figurative way. It is used in a literal sense in Luke 6:39, where Jesus asked, "Can the blind lead the blind?" Here in Acts 8:31 it is used in the figurative sense. The Ethiopian wanted Philip to guide him in understanding the passage from Isaiah. Another way to translate this word in this context is "explains" (NIV).

❖ *Search the Scriptures*

The Spirit of God led Philip to encounter the Ethiopian eunuch, who had been to Jerusalem to worship. The Ethiopian was reading from Isaiah 53. When Philip asked if he understood what he was reading, the man asked Philip to guide him in understanding. Philip began with that passage and told the Ethiopian of Jesus. When the man asked to be baptized, Philip baptized him on his profession of faith. The eunuch went on his way rejoicing, and Philip went to other places telling the good news.

To help us in witnessing to people—especially to those who are culturally different from us—we will examine four principles found in this passage.

Spiritual Sensitivity (Acts 8:26-29)

What shows Philip's spiritual sensitivity? In what ways was the Ethiopian eunuch culturally different from Philip? Was he a God-fearing Gentile or a Jewish proselyte? What barriers did each man cross for the Ethiopian to hear the good news?

Verses 26-29: And the angel of the Lord spake unto Philip, saying, Arise, and go toward the south unto the way that goeth down from Jerusalem unto Gaza, which is desert. [27]And he rose and went: and, behold, a man of Ethiopia, an eunuch of great authority under Candace queen of the Ethiopians, who had the charge of all her treasure, and had come to Jerusalem for to worship, [28]was returning, and sitting in his chariot read Isaiah the prophet. [29]Then the Spirit said unto Philip, Go near, and join thyself to this chariot.

Philip was not the apostle Philip but one of the seven chosen by the Jerusalem church to meet the needs of the Hellenistic widows (Acts 6:1-6). To distinguish him from the apostle, he often is called Philip the evangelist. When persecution broke out after the death of Stephen, Philip was one of those who was scattered abroad and went everywhere preaching the word (8:1-4). He went to Samaria and many Samaritans believed the good news of salvation in Christ (vv. 5-8). Jesus mentioned Samaria by name in His commission for His followers to be witnesses (1:8). Samaria was not far away; it was between Judea and Galilee. Jesus had made many converts on His visit there (John 4:1-42). Yet no Jewish believer had gone to the Samaritans until Philip went. When the apostles at Jerusalem heard about what was happening in Samaria, they sent Peter and John to see what was going on. These two also ended up preaching the good news to Samaritans (Acts 8:25).

Philip was in Samaria in this successful evangelistic campaign when **the angel of the Lord** delivered what must have seemed a strange message to Philip. Later in the account **the Spirit** was the One who directed Philip's movements. Both **the angel** and **the Spirit** were speaking for God. Philip showed his spiritual sensitivity by obeying any word from the Lord. He did not ask questions; he simply obeyed.

The angel told Philip, **Arise, and go toward the south unto the way that goeth down from Jerusalem unto Gaza, which is desert.** What would you have wanted to ask the Lord when the angel told you to leave a successful evangelistic campaign among the Samaritans, a group who desperately needed the good news, and go to a desolate road? Most of us would have wanted to know why the Lord was leading us from a successful venture to a road in the desert. **Gaza** was the last place to get water before the desert on the way to Egypt. The Lord did not explain to Philip why he was to do this, and apparently Philip did not ask. He simply **rose and went.** He trusted that the Lord had His reasons for such a command.

Verse 27 introduces another traveler on that road at the exact time Philip was. He was **a man of Ethiopia.** His country was south of Egypt between the first and sixth cataracts of the Nile. It should not be confused with modern Ethiopia, which is in the hill country to the east of the Upper Nile. This was probably the ancient kingdom of Meroe, also called the Nubian Empire and, in the Old Testament, the kingdom of Cush. The inhabitants were black. In fact, the Greek word from which the name Ethiopia came (*Aithiops*) meant "people with a burnt face." Ethiopia flourished between the eighth century B.C. and the fourth century A.D.

The man Philip met was a person **of great authority** (*dynastes*; "an important official," NIV). *Dynastes* is a word for power. He served **Candace queen of the Ethiopians. Candace** was a title, not a person's name. "The king of Ethiopia was venerated as the child of the sun and regarded as too sacred a personage to discharge the secular functions of royalty; these were performed on his behalf by the queen-mother, who bore the dynastic title Kandake."[3] The man whom Philip met **had the charge of all her treasure.** We probably would call him the minister of finance.

Eunuch in our language refers to a man who is physically a eunuch; but in ancient society the same word was also used at times to refer to a government official. The Hebrew word for eunuch, for example, was used of Potiphar, who was a married man (Gen. 39:1,7). The Greek word meant "one in charge of a bed," a reference to the use of literal eunuchs to guard harems. We do not know for sure whether this man was literally a eunuch or only a high official. Many Bible students think that he was a physical eunuch. John Polhill wrote, "It is likely that Philip's Ethiopian was an actual physical eunuch, however, since the terms 'eunuch' and 'official over the treasury' are both given."[4]

One factor that makes the eunuch's physical status important to this story is that the Old Testament placed restrictions on physical eunuchs. They could not be priests or even belong to the congregation of Israel (Lev. 21:20; Deut. 23:1). Isaiah 56:3-5 predicted a time when eunuchs could belong to the people of God. Luke told us that the eunuch **had come to Jerusalem for to worship.** This reference leads some Bible students to believe that this man was a proselyte to Judaism. More likely, the Ethiopian was a God-fearing Gentile like Cornelius. The fact that he was a eunuch seems decisive in coming to this conclusion. He believed in the God of the Jews, in the Jewish Scriptures, and he sought to worship God. His worship in Jerusalem was restricted to the court of the Gentiles, but he could worship there as best he could. When Philip saw him **sitting in his chariot** headed **south,** he **was returning** from Jerusalem. As the eunuch rode along, he was reading from **Isaiah the prophet. The Spirit** told **Philip** to **join** himself **to this chariot** ("stay near it," NIV).

What cultural differences were there between Philip and the Ethiopian? What barriers did he have to cross to tell the good news to the Ethiopian eunuch? What things did they have in common? They were from different nations, different social and economic groups, and different ethnic groups. They had in common belief in the same God, use of the same Scriptures, and knowledge of the same language. Greek was a universal language in the first century. Philip was about to cross the barriers and build on the things they had in common. Under normal conditions, a high official in the Ethiopian government would not invite a Jewish traveler to join him in his chariot. Nor would a faithful Jew have such close contact with a Gentile. But God was bringing them together for the sake of telling the eunuch the good news. For this to happen, both men would have to ignore barriers and build on what they had in common.

Scriptural Explanation (Acts 8:30-35)

Why did the Ethiopian ask Philip to come and sit by him? Why did Philip go? How did Philip take the initiative? How did the Ethiopian show his openness? What passage was the eunuch reading? Why was he confused? How did Philip take advantage of this opportunity?

Verses 30-35: **And Philip ran thither to him, and heard him read the prophet Isaiah, and said, Understandest thou what thou readest? 31And he said, How can I, except some man should guide me? And he desired Philip that he would come up and sit with him. 32The place of the scripture which he read was this, He was led as a sheep to the slaughter; and like a lamb dumb before his shearer, so opened he not his mouth: 33in his humiliation his judgment was taken away:**

and who shall declare his generation? for his life is taken from the earth. [34]And the eunuch answered Philip, and said, I pray thee, of whom speaketh the prophet this? of himself, or of some other man? [35]Then Philip opened his mouth, and began at the same scripture, and preached unto him Jesus.

Someone with less Christian faith and love might have failed to take advantage of this opportunity, but not Philip. When the Spirit told him to go near the chariot, he **ran** to do just that. No doubt he had been wondering why the Spirit had led him away from Samaria to this desert road. However, when he saw the Ethiopian and realized he was reading from the Scriptures, he was eager to take advantage of this God-given appointment. When he heard the passage being read, Philip knew this was the Lord's doing.

When the Spirit prompted Philip to go near the chariot, he heard what the man was reading. In those days, reading aloud was normal. The letters on ancient documents often were crowded and difficult to decipher, and a reader had to pick his way though a document. The eunuch probably was reading from a scroll. Philip took the initiative by asking the man, **Understandest thou what thou readest?** Philip's question contains a play on words in Greek. **Understandest** is *ginoskeis*; **readest** is the same word but with *ana* on the front, *anaginoskeis*.

The Ethiopian responded, **How can I, except some man should guide me?** Something about this fellow traveler prompted the eunuch to invite Philip to **come up and sit with him.** Not many high officials would pick up a solitary traveler from the common people. To the credit of the Ethiopian, he did not allow cultural differences to prevent him from inviting Philip to come and sit by him. He must have sensed from Philip's question that he could shed light on the words from Isaiah.

Philip discovered that the Ethiopian was reading in **the scripture** from what we call Isaiah 53, the Suffering Servant passage that was fulfilled in Jesus Christ (see Mark 10:45). Acts 8:32-33 is from the Greek translation of Isaiah 53:7-8. These verses describe someone who **was led as a sheep to the slaughter; and like a lamb dumb before his shearer, so opened he not his mouth.** He was in a state of **humiliation** in which "he was deprived of justice" (NIV). These words describe the silence of Jesus in the face of the cruel and unjust way He was treated. Jesus was called the Lamb of God (John 1:29).

The question **Who shall declare his generation?** may mean "that his life was cut off short or perhaps the opposite, that the tragedy of his death had been followed by a whole host of disciples who had come to believe and trust in him."[5] His death is described in the words **his life is taken from the earth.**

The Ethiopian eunuch showed good insight when he asked, **Of whom speaketh the prophet this? of himself, or of some other man?** Fortunately, Philip was a student of the Scriptures as interpreted by Jesus after His resurrection. What a tragedy if he had to admit that he did not know the answer to the eunuch's questions! But Philip did know who was being described in Isaiah 53. Therefore, he told his traveling companion the good news about **Jesus.**

Verse 35 makes three important points: First of all, Philip had something important to say. The words **opened his mouth** introduced important messages (see Matt. 5:2; Acts 10:34). Second, what he said was based on the Word of God. With Isaiah open before them, Philip **began at the same scripture.** Third, what he had to say was focused on the good news of Jesus. The Greek word for **preached** here is *euengelisato,* which means "told him the good news" (NIV). In other words, this is not something only preachers should be able to do; it is something all Christians should be able to do—tell others about Jesus. He told him the good news about **Jesus.** We are not told all that Philip said, but we are told the heart of what he said. Philip told the eunuch of Jesus. Probably Philip told him much of what Peter said at Pentecost. Since Philip **began** with Isaiah 53, he surely told him about the death of Jesus.

What an opportunity Philip had! The Ethiopian was a seeker of truth. The Bible was opened to Isaiah 53. The man asked Philip a question that set him up for Philip to tell him the good news about Jesus. Although there were some real cultural differences between Philip and the eunuch, Philip and the eunuch ignored them, and Philip built on their common ground.

Missionaries and all Christian witnesses are wise to look for some common ground from which to point people to Jesus. Yet even if there is nothing more than our common humanity, we can tell the good news of Jesus Christ. All who tell the good news look forward to meeting someone like the eunuch whose heart is ready for the message of Christ.

Significant Questions (Acts 8:36-38)

What is the significance of the question the eunuch asked Philip? What was the significance of the question asked by Philip? What is the significance of the Ethiopian's answer to Philip's question? What does verse 38 teach about baptism?

Verses 36-38: And as they went on their way, they came unto a certain water: and the eunuch said, See, here is water; what doth hinder me to be baptized? [37]And Philip said, If thou believest with all thine heart, thou mayest. And he answered and said, I believe that Jesus Christ is the Son of God. [38]And he commanded the chariot to stand still: and they went down both into the water, both Philip and the eunuch; and he baptized him.

A lot was said between verses 35 and 36 that was not recorded. Apparently Philip told the Ethiopian about baptism. The Ethiopian asked about being baptized when they came to some **water.** The wording of the eunuch's question is important: **What doth hinder me to be baptized?;** "Why shouldn't I be baptized?" (NIV); "What is to prevent me from being baptized?" (NRSV). The word translated **hinder** is *koluei.* Peter used the same verb in 10:47 and 11:17, both of which have to do with being baptized. The Ethiopian eunuch may have had in mind the fact that his being a eunuch hindered his becoming a convert to Judaism. Peter used this word to refer to the hindrances that Jews placed on Gentiles who wanted to fully practice the Jewish religion. It may be significant that the last word in the Greek text of Acts is *akolutos,* which means "unhindered" (28:31).

Verse 38 shows that Philip baptized the man. Many translations do not include verse 37 because it is not in the earliest and most reliable manuscripts of Acts. John Polhill noted that verse 37 "has considerable value. It seems to embody a very early Christian baptismal confession where the one baptizing asked the candidate if he believed in Christ with all his heart, to which the candidate would respond by confessing Jesus Christ as the Son of God."[6]

Philip must have either asked such a question or in some other way made sure that the man was trusting the Lord with all his heart. The Ethiopian would made such a verbal confession before Philip baptized him. The Ethiopian **commanded the chariot to stand still: and they went down both into the water, both Philip and the eunuch; and he baptized him.** The word *baptizo* means "to immerse" or "to dip." Baptism of a believer by immersion is not only a confession of faith but also a portrayal of death and resurrection. In the Great Commission of Matthew 28:18-20, Jesus included baptism among the steps in making disciples. The goal of Christian missions is to make disciples.

Spiritual Transformation (Acts 8:39-40)

*How was Philip **caught away**? What happened to the eunuch? What happened to Philip?*

Verses 39-40: And when they were come up out of the water, the Spirit of the Lord caught away Philip, that the eunuch saw him no more: and he went on his way rejoicing. ⁴⁰But Philip was found at Azotus: and passing through he preached in all the cities, till he came to Caesarea.

After coming **up out of the water, the Spirit of the Lord caught away Philip.** The Holy Spirit is referred to in a variety of ways. **The Spirit of the Lord** emphasizes this as the ongoing work of the Lord Jesus Christ. Throughout the Book of Acts, emphasis is placed on the work of the Spirit. He had led Philip and the eunuch to meet while the latter was reading Isaiah 53. He had used the testimony of Philip to win the eunuch. Now He had another mission for Philip. **Caught away** is *herpasen,* which can be translated "snatched . . . away" (NRSV). This seems to imply that the Lord quickly took Philip from one place to another.

The Ethiopian eunuch, however, was not disturbed by Philip's departure, as **he went on his way rejoicing.** The eunuch was no longer excluded but included among the people of God. The Bible does not tell us what happened when he arrived in his homeland. Some ancient traditions say that he told the good news there.

Meanwhile, what was Philip doing? **Philip was found at Azotus** [uh-ZOH-tuhs]: **and passing through he preached in all the cities.** In other words, he witnessed for the Lord as he went on his way. Philip was one who witnessed wherever he went and to whomever he met. He did not let human barriers hinder him from telling the good news. He had the heart of a missionary.

Philip arrived in **Caesarea,** where he seems to have settled down. Years later, when Paul passed through this area, he "entered into the house of Philip the evangelist, which was one of the seven; and abode with him. And the same man had four daughters, virgins, which did prophesy" (21:8-9).

Philip was an evangelist and a missionary. He told the good news near and far, and he told it to people of different cultures. One does not have to go to a foreign land to find people of cultures other than one's own. Our own country is a mixture of racial and ethnic groups, and people from other cultures come to our land for many reasons.

Often international students are more open to a gospel witness when they are away from their native culture. When they return home, they take the good news of Jesus with them.

❖ *Spiritual Transformations*

The Lord led Philip to cross paths with the Ethiopian when he was reading Isaiah 53. Although cultural barriers separated the two men, Philip used the meeting as an opportunity to tell the Ethiopian the good news of Jesus. The eunuch asked what hindered him from being baptized, and Philip baptized him after hearing his confession of faith. The Ethiopian found new joy, and Philip was led to other places to tell the good news.

This familiar biblical account can be applied in many ways: how to witness, how to use the Bible in witnessing, how to be sensitive to the Lord's leadership, and how to identify those who are seeking the Lord. This lesson focuses on this story to emphasize that missionary work involves taking the good news across cultural barriers. People specially called to be missionaries are called to this work—either overseas or at home. All Christians are called to be witnesses, and we act as missionaries when we cross cultural barriers with the good news.

*What people with whom you come in contact are in a cultural group different from your own?*_____

What are you doing to see that the good news is told to people of all people groups? _____

Prayer of Commitment: Lord, help me be sensitive to the Spirit's leadership in telling the good news to all people.

[1]Jerry Rankin as quoted in William R. Estep, *Whole Gospel Whole World* [Nashville: Broadman & Holman Publishers, 1994], 381.

[2]R. Alton James, "Turbulent and Transitional: The Story of Missions in the Twentieth Century," in *Missiology: An Introduction to the Foundations, History, and Strategies of World Missions,* edited by John Mark Terry, Ebbie Smith, and Justice Anderson, [Nashville: Broadman & Holman Publishers, 1998], 258-259.

[3]F. F. Bruce, *The Book of the Acts,* revised edition, in the New International Commentary on the New Testament [Grand Rapids: William B. Eerdmans Publishing Company, 1988], 175.

[4]Polhill, "Acts," NAC, 224.

[5]Polhill, "Acts," NAC, 225.

[6]Polhill, "Acts," NAC, 226.

Obedience to God's Call

Background Passage: Acts 13:1-52; 14:26-27
Focal Passage: Acts 13:1-6a,13-16,47-48; 14:26-27
Key Verse: Acts 13:47

❖ *Significance of the Lesson*

• The *Theme* of this lesson is that because God wants all people to receive the good news about Jesus, some people go to other places to tell others about Him.

• The *Life Question* addressed in this lesson is, Where does God want to use me to tell other people the good news about Jesus?

• The *Biblical Truth* is that God sets apart some believers to go across geographic and cultural boundaries to tell the lost about Jesus.

• The *Life Impact* is to help you be obedient to whatever God shows you to do to tell the peoples of the world the good news about Jesus.

Attitudes About Missionaries and Missions Work

In a secular worldview, Christian missionary work is either ignored or criticized. Many secular people criticize missionaries for trying to impose another culture and religion on people with their own culture and religion. Secular people assume that one religion is as good as another, and no religion may be even better.

In the biblical worldview, God calls all believers to tell the good news; and He calls some to go as missionaries to other lands. Dedicated Christians believe strongly in world missions. They pray for missionaries, give to support missionary work, and pray for the Lord to send forth workers in fields "white already to harvest" (John 4:35). Some Christians feel that God is calling them to go as missionaries—either as career missionaries or in short-term missionary work.

Word Study: *Called*

Called (*proskeklemai*) is a key word in Acts 13:2. The word is used of God's call of Barnabas and Saul to become missionaries. Further, the word is in the perfect tense, meaning that the church did not originate the call; the church only recognized and affirmed the inner call the Holy Spirit already had issued to Barnabas and Saul.

❖ *Search the Scriptures*

Barnabas and Saul were called to be missionaries, and the Antioch church sent them out. They went first to Cyprus and then to Antioch of Pisidia, where in both places they preached first in the synagogues; but they also told the good news to Gentiles. They fulfilled the Lord's command to be a light to the Gentiles, resulting in the salvation and rejoicing of many Gentiles. At the end of their first journey, they reported to the Antioch church what the Lord had done through them.

The focus of this lesson is on *where* to tell the good news. The emphasis is that some people go to faraway places to tell others the good news. Concerning this we will observe four points.

The Call and the Commission (Acts 13:1-3)

In what ways was the Antioch church a good model for what a church should be? Who were the ones whose actions are described in verses 2-3? What was distinctive about what is described in verses 1-3? How does a person recognize a call to be a missionary?

13:1: Now there were in the church that was at Antioch certain prophets and teachers; as Barnabas, and Simeon that was called Niger, and Lucius of Cyrene, and Manaen, which had been brought up with Herod the tetrarch, and Saul.

The church that was at Antioch, described in Acts 11:19-30, is a good example of what a church should be and do. The church was begun when unnamed Jewish believers were scattered by Saul's persecution. Some of them came to Antioch where they preached first to fellow Jews but also began to preach to Gentiles, many of whom believed. The Jerusalem church sent Barnabas to see what was happening. This openhearted man encouraged the new church in its inclusion of Gentile believers. Barnabas brought the converted Saul to help in teaching the people. When the Antioch church heard that Jewish believers were facing a famine, they sent an offering (vv. 27-30).

Another vital move by the Antioch church is described in Acts 13:1-3. This church became the first truly missionary church. "What is new to these chapters is that for the first time a local Christian church was led to see the need for a witness beyond them to the larger world and commissioned missionaries to carry out that task."[1]

Five key leaders of the church were called **prophets and teachers.** We are familiar with two of these: **Barnabas** and **Saul.** All we know about the others is found in verse 1. **Simeon that was called Niger** was probably black. Some have speculated whether he was Simon of Cyrene, who was ordered by Roman soldiers to carry Jesus' cross; however, this is unlikely. **Lucius of Cyrene** is thought by some to be Luke the physician, who wrote the Gospel of Luke and the Book of Acts. This also is unlikely. **Manaen** [MAN-uh-en], **which had been brought up with Herod the tetrarch,** had grown up with Herod Antipas, although what this means is not spelled out.

We do know much about **Barnabas** and about **Saul. Barnabas** is mentioned first when he sold a field and brought the money to the apostles to help others. His name was Joseph. Barnabas, which means "son of encouragement," was a nickname (4:36-37). The name stuck because Barnabas was an encourager. After Saul's conversion, Barnabas alone stood up for the former persecutor when Saul came to the Jerusalem church (9:27). He also encouraged the Antioch church in its inclusion of Gentile believers (11:22-24).

Saul was the leader of the persecution after the death of Stephen (8:1-4). He was fanatical in his hatred of the believers in Jesus. Then he met the Lord on the Damascus road, and his life was changed. Under the Lord's leadership and with help and encouragement from Barnabas, Saul went on to become the strongest advocate for salvation by grace through faith, which was offered to all people. Saul was at Antioch because Barnabas had sought him and brought him from Tarsus to help teach the new believers at Antioch.

13:2-3: **As they ministered to the Lord, and fasted, the Holy Ghost** [Spirit] **said, Separate me Barnabas and Saul for the work whereunto I have called them. [3]And when they had fasted and prayed, and laid their hands on them, they sent them away.**

To whom does the word **they** refer in verse 2? Does the word refer only to the five leaders mentioned in verse 1, or does it refer to the entire congregation? Verse 1 mentions both. Many Bible students think that a stronger case can be made for the church as a whole.

The word **ministered** translates *leitourgounton,* a word that originally referred to people who served the public at their own expense. It was used in the Greek Old Testament to refer to the kind of service done by the priests and Levites in the temple. In the New Testament it was the kind of service performed in worship. Thus it is usually translated as "worshiping" (NIV).

They also **fasted.** This shows how fasting provides a setting in which people are more open to hear the will of God. While they were worshiping the Lord and fasting, the Holy Spirit spoke to them.

The message from the Spirit was, **Separate me** ("set apart for me," NIV) **Barnabas and Saul for the work whereunto I have called them.** When Saul met the Lord on the Damascus road, the Lord revealed that Saul was to be a witness to Gentiles (9:15; 22:21; 26:16-17). The missionary work that followed this call shows that Paul became the leader in taking the good news to Gentiles. Thus they were called to be missionaries.

The urban area of Antioch was filled with Gentiles; therefore, someone might have objected to the church's sending their two best leaders off to find Gentiles who needed to hear the good news. They had barely scratched the surface in Antioch. But the Lord revealed in His call to Barnabas and Saul that they were to go to other places to tell people the good news.

The church at Antioch **fasted and prayed.** They confirmed that the Spirit was indeed leading these two choice leaders to take the good news to other places and people. Therefore, the church commissioned them. When they **laid their hands on** Barnabas and Saul, they were setting them aside to fulfill the work to which God was calling them. They were not ordaining them so much as commissioning them. After doing this, **they sent them away.** The Greek word is *apelusan.* This word has the idea of releasing or letting go. The *New English Bible* reads "let them go." If this was the meaning, *apelusan* refers to setting them free from their leadership roles in the church. However, **sent them away** is a good translation because the church was not a passive bystander; instead, the church was involved in the process of the call to Barnabas and Saul, and the church sent them out with their blessing.

Called (*proskeklemai*) is a key word here. This word and its related compound forms are used in several ways in the Bible. Sometimes the *call* refers to the calling to Christ that comes to all believers. All Christians are called to live in a way worthy of their calling (Eph. 4:1). Sometimes the word *call* is used of God's call to some specific task. This was true of Barnabas and Saul. They were called to be missionaries. "The missionary call is a specific role given to some to share Christ with the unreached peoples of the world."[2]

The Mission and the Missionaries (Acts 13:4-6a,13-16)

What is the role of the Holy Spirit in missionary work? Where did Barnabas and Saul go on their first missionary journey? Why did they first go to a synagogue? What was John Mark supposed to do? Why did he leave the missionary team? What leadership change took place on Cyprus? What groups did Paul address in Antioch of Pisidia?

13:4-6a: So they, being sent forth by the Holy Ghost [Spirit], departed unto Seleucia; and from thence they sailed to Cyprus. [5]And when they were at Salamis, they preached the word of God in the synagogues of the Jews: and they had also John to their minister. [6a]And . . . they had gone through the isle unto Paphos.

Barnabas and Saul were **sent forth by the Holy Ghost** ("sent on their way by the Holy Spirit," NIV). The Holy Spirit was the One who called them, and He was the One who sent them out.

Seleucia [sih-LYOO-shih-uh] was the seaport town that served Antioch of Syria. **Cyprus** is a large island in the eastern Mediterranean. **Salamis** [SAL-uh-miss] was the closest port of Cyprus coming from Seleucia. Barnabas was from Cyprus. This was the first place visited by the missionary team.

Barnabas and Saul began their mission to Cyprus by preaching **the word of God in the synagogues of the Jews.** This became a missionary strategy wherever they went. The synagogues provided a logical starting point for Jewish-Christian missionaries. The missionaries and the Jews had in common a belief in the same God and in the same Scriptures. The Jews were looking for the Messiah. The missionaries could preach Jesus as the Messiah.

In the statement **they had also John,** the reference is to John Mark, Barnabas's kinsman (Col. 4:10). Mark, as we know him better, was from Jerusalem. His mother's name was Mary, and the Jerusalem church met in their house (Acts 12:12). When Barnabas and Saul returned to Antioch after delivering an offering from the Antioch church, John Mark had come with them (12:25). Now we learn that John Mark had come with them on this missionary journey. We do not know what was his role on the missionary team. He is called a

minister ("helper," NIV; "assistant," NKJV). He may have had duties teaching new converts the basics of the faith. He may have come along to do whatever was needed and to learn in the process.

13:13-16: **Now when Paul and his company loosed from Paphos, they came to Perga in Pamphylia: and John departing from them returned to Jerusalem.** [14]**But when they departed from Perga, they came to Antioch in Pisidia, and went into the synagogue on the sabbath day, and sat down.** [15]**And after the reading of the law and the prophets the rulers of the synagogue sent unto them, saying, Ye men and brethren, if ye have any word of exhortation for the people, say on.** [16]**Then Paul stood up, and beckoning with his hand said, Men of Israel, and ye that fear God, give audience.**

The missionaries worked their way to the other side of the island and ended up at **Paphos** [PAY-fahs]. This was the seat of the Roman government in Cyprus. Verses 6b-12 tell how Sergius Paulus, the Roman proconsul, was won to faith in Jesus Christ. While they were in Cyprus, a significant change in leadership took place. When they went to Cyprus, the name of Barnabas was mentioned before Saul (see v. 7). While they were there, Luke mentions that Saul became known as **Paul.** And when the missionaries left Cyprus, they were called **Paul and his company** (v. 13). Paul continued to be the leader during the rest of that missionary journey.

This change apparently was done with the cooperation of Barnabas. This big-hearted man saw the potential of Saul from the beginning. Barnabas stood up for Saul at Jerusalem. He summoned him to help at Antioch. Now he stepped aside to allow Paul to become leader. This change, however, could have been a factor in John Mark's decision to leave the missionary team. When they left **Paphos** [PAY-fahs] in Cyprus, they went to **Perga** [PUHR-guh] **in Pamphylia** [pam-FIL-ih-uh], on the southern coast of Asia Minor. At that point, **John departing from them returned to Jerusalem.**

Several theories have been proposed to explain why John Mark left them. He may have become homesick. Missionary work usually involves culture shock. Mark may have reacted by going home. He may have not agreed with Paul's emphasis on going to Gentiles. This may have been coupled with resentment over Paul's replacing his relative Barnabas as leader. We are not told why he left, but we do know certain facts: Paul later thought of Mark as a deserter, and he refused Barnabas's suggestion to take Mark on their second journey. As a result, the team split up—Paul taking Silas and Barnabas taking Mark (15:36-41). Years later, Paul recognized that Mark had become a useful servant of Christ (Col. 4:10).

The missionaries journeyed over 100 miles north over the Taurus Mountains **to Antioch in Pisidia.** The missionaries followed their strategy of going first to the local **synagogue.** We see in verse 15 **the reading of the law and the prophets. The rulers of the synagogue** were in charge of the order of service. They apparently recognized Paul as a rabbi and said to the visitors, **If ye have any word of exhortation for the people, say on.**

This must have been the opportunity Paul was praying for. He **stood up, and beckoning with his hand said, Men of Israel, ye that fear God, give audience.** Notice that he addressed not only the Jews **(men of Israel)** but also the God-fearing Gentiles **(ye that fear God).**

Many people groups or groups with distinctive cultures have not heard the good news. Many of these can be reached only as people go to them with the good news of Jesus. Those who go may be career missionaries, but some may be military personnel, businessmen and businesswomen, or tourists who are in contact with people groups who have not heard the good news. Many of the people groups are in lands closed to formal missionaries; in such cases, non-missionaries become especially important.

The Message and the Response (Acts 13:47-48)

*How does verse 47 show the Old Testament doctrine of missions? Who fulfilled this prophecy? What was the response of the Gentiles to Paul's sermon? In what sense were those who believed **ordained to eternal life**?*

13:47-48: For so hath the Lord commanded us, saying, I have set thee to be a light of the Gentiles, that thou shouldest be for salvation unto the ends of the earth. [48]And when the Gentiles heard this, they were glad, and glorified the word of the Lord: and as many as were ordained to eternal life believed.

Paul's sermon in verses 17-41 has much in common with Peter's sermon on the day of Pentecost. The themes are that the Old Testament promises are fulfilled in Christ. He was crucified, but God raised Him from the dead. Through Him, forgiveness and justification are offered to those who place their faith in Him. Many of the Jews and

Jewish proselytes responded positively to Paul's message and asked him to preach again on the next Sabbath. By then, however, the hearts of many of the Jews were hardened, and Paul told them, "It was necessary that the word of God should first have been spoken to you: but seeing ye put it from you, and judge yourselves unworthy of everlasting life, lo, we turn to the Gentiles" (v. 46).

Paul then quoted Isaiah 49:6 to show God's intention to include the Gentiles and to refer to the call of Christ for missionaries to be **a light** that brings the offer of **salvation unto the ends of the earth.** This latter point is seen in Paul's introduction of this quotation: **For so hath the Lord commanded us.** When the Lord called Saul of Tarsus, He said that He was sending Saul "to open their eyes, and to turn them from darkness to light" (Acts 26:18). When Jesus was presented in the temple as an infant, Simeon had quoted a similar passage as fulfilled in Jesus (Luke 2:30-32). Jesus certainly is the Light of the world (John 8:12). However, in Matthew 5:14 Jesus said that His followers are also the light of the world. We are light in the sense of reflecting His light.

Luke recorded that **when the Gentiles heard this, they were glad, and glorified the word of the Lord.** This joyful response is similar to the Samaritans' and the Ethiopian's responses after Philip preached the good news to them (8:8,39).

As many as were ordained ("appointed," NIV, NKJV; "destined," NRSV) **to eternal life believed. Ordained** translates *tetagmenoi.* This verb has several possible meanings: "be appointed to something," "be assigned to a certain classification," or "be classed among those possessing something." When Christians seek to trace back their salvation to its source, it leads back to the loving heart of the eternal God. Kenneth O. Gangel gave this illustration that he heard from Alva J. McLain: "He described a gate into the garden of salvation. Over the outside portal one reads the words *Whosoever will may come. . . .* What shock to discover that the words on the inside portal are different: *Chosen in him from the foundation of the world.*"[3]

The Return and the Report (Acts 14:26-27)

Why did Paul and Barnabas return to Antioch of Syria? What report did they give? How can churches today receive reports from missionaries?

14:26-27: And thence sailed to Antioch, from whence they had been recommended to the grace of God for the work which they

fulfilled. [27]And when they were come, and had gathered the church together, they rehearsed all that God had done with them, and how he had opened the door of faith unto the Gentiles.

Persecution forced Paul and Barnabas to leave Antioch in Pisidia; they visited Iconium [eye-KOH-nih-uhm], Lystra, and Derbe. They were persecuted in each place, and in Lystra Paul was stoned and left for dead. Yet Paul went back through each city on his way back to the church that had sent them out. They arrived back in **Antioch** of Syria and to the church that had **recommended** them **to the grace of God for** ("been placed in God's care for," CEV) **the work which they fulfilled.** They **gathered the church together.** Then **they rehearsed** ("reported," NIV, NKJV) **all that God had done with them. With** is the usual meaning of *meta*. If it has that meaning here, the emphasis is on their cooperation with God in doing His work. If the meaning is "through" (NIV, NEB, REB), the emphasis is on this being God's work and them being used by Him. In either case, what they did was done under the direction and in the power of God's Spirit.

The obvious conclusion of their work was that the Lord **had opened the door of faith unto the Gentiles.** Some fellow Jewish Christians challenged this conclusion, and the Jerusalem Conference was held (see Acts 15:1-35). The result was an endorsement by the church of the work of Paul and Barnabas.

This passage shows the importance of missionaries reporting on their work to the church or churches that commissioned them. This is important so that the churches can pray for and support the work of the missionaries.

Southern Baptists have effective and efficient ways of supporting missionaries commissioned through the International Mission Board in the Cooperative Program and in The Lottie Moon Christmas Offering for International Missions. Some churches have missionaries from their own church, but many churches are helping support missionaries from other churches that are sent forth with the prayers and support of all the churches.

However, churches need ways of personalizing international missions work. Here are some suggestions:

• Participate in missions conferences where you can meet missionaries.

• Use the prayer calendar to pray daily for specific missionaries.

• Pray that the Lord will call forth missionaries from your church.

• Read *The Commission* magazine and other missions education materials.

- Volunteer for short-term missionary work. Call the International Mission Board at 1-800-888-VOLS (1-800-888-8657).
- Provide a missionary house for missionaries on state-side assignment.
- "Adopt a Missionary." This program is sponsored by the International Mission Board and is designed to enable a church to stay in touch with and support a specific missionary. For additional information, call 1-800-362-1322.
- Work with your pastor to invite a missionary on state-side assignment to speak at your church.

❖ *Spiritual Transformations*

When the Lord called Barnabas and Saul, the Antioch church commissioned them and sent them out. They went to various places and told the good news of Christ to Gentiles as well as to Jews. In doing so, they reflected the light Jesus had come to bring to a sin-darkened world. The missionaries returned to the church that had commissioned them and reported what God had done through them.

God calls all believers to be witnesses where they are, and He calls some to become missionaries. He leads missionaries to cross not only geographic boundaries but also cultural barriers. God works through missionaries to fulfill His eternal purpose for all people to hear the good news. Missionaries need to report to churches on the work that God has done through them.

How have you responded to opportunities to cross cultural barriers to tell the good news about Jesus? _____

How can you learn more about the missionaries commissioned and sent forth through the International Mission Board? _____

Have you ever participated in a short-term, volunteer missions project? If not, what would it take for the Lord to get you to do so?

_____

Prayer of Commitment: Lord, help me to do my part in fulfilling the Great Commission, even if it means going to faraway places and to people of other cultures. Amen.

[1]Polhill, "Acts," NAC, 288.
[2]Bill Goff, "Missionary Call and Service," in *Missiology*, 335.
[3]Kenneth O. Gangel, *Acts*, in the Holman New Testament Commentary [Nashville: Broadman & Holman Publishers, 1998], 224-225.

Reasons to Tell the Good News

Background Passage: Acts 17:16-34
Focal Passage: Acts 17:16-31
Key Verse: Acts 17:16

❖ *Significance of the Lesson*

• The *Theme* of this lesson is that not everyone knows the good news about Jesus.

• The *Life Question* this lesson seeks to address is, Why should I be concerned about making certain all people have an opportunity to respond to the good news?

• The *Biblical Truth* is that people without Christ are lost and need to respond to the good news by repenting and believing in Jesus.

• The *Life Impact* is to help you share the good news about Jesus in all situations so people will come to know and love Him.

Christianity and Other Religions

Secular worldviews allow many gods. Few of those trapped in humanism and materialism are aware of their gods. Truly secular people profess no religion and feel that all religions are useless. They do not believe that Christianity is the only way to God. They believe that if there is a God, He will send no one to hell.

In the biblical worldview, people without Christ are lost. Believers are responsible for sharing the good news of Christ with all people—including those who claim to have no religious beliefs and those who are adherents of other religions. Many professing Christians are more in tune with the world's view than they are the biblical view on this matter.

Word Study: *Wholly given to idolatry*

The usual word for *idol* is *eidolon*. The word Paul used in Acts 17:16 translated "wholly given to idolatry" or "full of idols" (NIV; *kateidolos*) occurs nowhere else in the New Testament and has not been found in any other Greek literature. John Stott wrote, "Although most English versions render it 'full of idols,' the idea conveyed seems to be that the city was 'under' them. We might say that it was 'smothered with idols' or 'swamped' by them. Alternatively, since *kata* words often express luxurious growth, what Paul saw was 'a veritable forest of idols.'"[1]

❖ *Search the Scriptures*

While Paul was in Athens, he went to the synagogue and to the marketplace to tell others about Jesus. When the Epicurean and Stoic philosophers heard him telling the good news, they were curious enough to ask him to speak to the council. Paul made known the unknown God by speaking about the divine Creator and His desire to know people. When Paul spoke about judgment, resurrection, and the need for them to repent, most of them laughed at him; but some believed.

In this lesson we will look at four reasons believers are to tell others the good news about Jesus.

People Are Lost (Acts 17:16-17)

Why was Paul by himself in Athens? Where and to whom did he witness? What does it mean to be lost?

Verses 16-17: Now while Paul waited for them at Athens, his spirit was stirred in him, when he saw the city wholly given to idolatry. [17]Therefore disputed he in the synagogue with the Jews, and with the devout persons, and in the market daily with them that met with him.

The visit to Athens took place on Paul's second missionary journey. Paul had been in Macedonia after seeing the vision of the man of Macedonia (Acts 16:9-10). He had preached in Philippi, Thessalonica, and Berea. In each city he encountered strong opposition. Paul left Silas and Timothy in Macedonia (17:15-16) while he went on to **Athens. Paul waited for them** there, but he was not just passing the time as he waited. He was actively involved in witnessing for Christ. As he usually did, he went to **the synagogue** and **disputed** ("reasoned," NIV) . . . **with the Jews, and with the devout persons.** These were the same two groups he found in most synagogues. The latter were God-fearing Gentiles.

Paul also witnessed **in the market daily with them that met with him** ("in the marketplace day by day with those who happened to be there," NIV). The marketplace was the *agora*, which was the hub of life in the city. Paul thus made himself available in a place where he could meet all kinds of people.

Athens had a noble past. Although its days of glory were in the past, the monuments of the past were still there. There were beautiful buildings and statues. Many tourists came to Athens to see these things. Paul was not there as a tourist but as a Christian missionary. Therefore, when he saw the buildings and statues, he was aware that the people honored various idols. This was why **his spirit was stirred in him. Stirred** translates *paroxuneto.* This is a strong word expressing deep emotion. It may be translated "greatly distressed" (NIV) or "deeply distressed" (NRSV). Paul was angry because these people had a heritage of a religion that deluded them and kept them in their lost condition, without the true and living God. Paul's actions, like his words, show that he believed that people without Christ are lost.

People Need to Hear the Good News (Acts 17:18-21)

*What did the **Epicureans** believe? What did the **Stoics** believe? What did they think of Paul and what He taught? Was **Areopagus** a place or a council? What did they think Paul meant by **Jesus, and the resurrection**? Why were they always seeking **some new thing**? Why are intellectuals often a hard group to reach with the good news? Why did Paul feel an obligation to tell the good news?*

Verses 18-21: Then certain philosophers of the Epicureans, and of the Stoics, encountered him. And some said, What will this babbler say? other some, He seemeth to be a setter forth of strange gods: because he preached unto them Jesus, and the resurrection. [19]And they took him, and brought him unto Areopagus, saying, May we know what this new doctrine, whereof thou speakest, is? [20]For thou bringest certain strange things to our ears: we would know therefore what these things mean. [21](For all the Athenians and strangers which were there spent their time in nothing else, but either to tell, or to hear some new thing.)

Among those whom Paul met were **certain philosophers.** These were the intellectuals of that time. Paul mentions two groups. **Epicureans** took their name from their founder Epicurus (died 270 B.C.), who taught that the purpose of life is the pursuit of pleasure. They sought a life free from pain, passion, and fear. Although the pleasure they sought was not always sensual pleasure, the common people often turned this philosophy into "Let us eat and drink; for tomorrow we die" (1 Cor. 15:32). Epicureans were materialists. They were not religious, believing if any gods existed, they had left the earth to run on its own.

Stoics emphasized reason and self-control. Their founder, Zeno (died 263 B.C.) believed the world was governed by fate. Religion was not important, but they believed that everything and everyone has some deity. In other words, they were pantheists. They were determined to live by reason, however painful that might be. Their goal was to be so detached from their surroundings that they were self-sufficient.

These intellectuals did not know what to make of Paul and his message. Like many intellectuals, they looked on any outsider in a less than flattering way. They called Paul a **babbler.** The word *spermologos* means "seed-picker." The image is of a bird pecking seeds from the ground.

For his part, "Paul was preaching the good news about Jesus and the resurrection" (NIV). **Preached** is the word *euengelizeto,* which means "to proclaim the good news." The content of Paul's proclamation was **Jesus, and the resurrection.** The philosophers, however, did not understand. They thought Paul was talking about two **strange gods.** This probably means they thought that **Jesus** (*Iesous*) was the name of the male deity and **resurrection** (*Anastasia*) was the female deity—like the Greek god Zeus and his wife Hera.

They led Paul to **Areopagus** [ehr-ih-AHP-uh-guhs]. This means "House of Ares," referring to the Greek god of war. Thus the name in verse 22 is "Mars' hill." Mars was the Roman counterpart of Ares. Originally this referred to a hill in Athens. Since the place later was the meeting place for a court or council, it is uncertain whether the hill or the council is meant in Acts 17. Most translations assume that it was the council. The *New International Version* calls it "a meeting of the Areopagus." Why did they bring Paul to this place? The setting does not seem to be a trial so much as a request for Paul to explain more clearly what he was teaching. They had more curiosity than interest. Luke told us that these philosophers **spent their time in nothing else, but either to tell, or to hear some new thing.**

Intellectuals are often one of the hardest groups to penetrate with the good news of Christ. They have an intellectual pride in their own ideas, and they often view religions as unfounded superstition. This is not a universal rule because some of the greatest advocates of the Christian faith have been intellectuals. Paul, for example, was a well-educated man who could hold his own with any group. Augustine,

Luther, Calvin, and C. S. Lewis were intellectuals who defended and proclaimed the Christian faith. One of the things needed in our day is more intellectuals to stand up for the Christian faith.

All believers ought to be able to tell why we believe. The apostle Peter wrote, "Be ready always to give an answer to every man that asketh you a reason of the hope that is in you with meekness and fear" (1 Pet. 3:15). Charles Colson wrote: "If our culture is to be transformed, it will happen from the bottom up—from ordinary believers practicing apologetics over the backyard fence or around the barbecue grill. To be sure, it's important for Christian scholars to conduct research and hold academic symposia, but the real leverage for cultural change comes from transforming the habits and dispositions of ordinary people."[2]

People Need to Be Introduced to the One True God (Acts 17:22-28)

*Why did Paul call them **too superstitious**? Why did he mention the altar **TO THE UNKNOWN GOD**? Why did Paul use different content in this sermon than he used in preaching in the synagogues? What truths about divine creation did he mention? Why did he quote from pagan poets? Why is there only one way to the one true God?*

Verses 22-23: Then Paul stood in the midst of Mars' hill, and said, Ye men of Athens, I perceive that in all things ye are too superstitious. [23]For as I passed by, and beheld your devotions, I found an altar with this inscription, TO THE UNKNOWN GOD. Whom therefore ye ignorantly worship, him declare I unto you.

Paul tried to get the attention of his listeners in two ways. For one thing, he called the idol worshipers **too superstitious.** The word *deisidaimonesterous* can also be translated "very religious" (NIV, NKJV; "extremely religious," HCSB). The word is ambiguous enough to have both negative and positive meanings. Would Paul begin by insulting them by calling them **superstitious**? More likely, he was trying to ease into his message by finding something good to say about them.

Paul explained his conclusion by referring to an **inscription** that he observed on one of the many altars in Athens. This shows that Paul had walked around the city. There were all kinds of shrines, altars, and statues of many gods. This **altar** and inscription was memorable to Paul because it was devoted **TO THE UNKNOWN GOD.** Apparently in their zeal to please all the gods, the people honored all the gods about whom they had heard. Just to be sure they had not missed one, they dedicated an altar to a God whose name they did not know.

Paul referred to this altar by announcing that he was about to tell them about this God whom they **ignorantly** worshiped. He was going to tell them about the one true God, whom they did not know. Many people do not know the one true God. Christians can and must make known to them the true God.

Verses 24-28: God that made the world and all things therein, seeing that he is Lord of heaven and earth, dwelleth not in temples made with hands; [25]neither is worshiped with men's hands, as though he needed anything, seeing he giveth to all life and breath, and all things; [26]and hath made of one blood all nations of men for to dwell on all the face of the earth, and hath determined the times before appointed, and the bounds of their habitation; [27]that they should seek the Lord, if haply they might feel after him, and find him, though he be not far from everyone of us: [28]For in him we live, and move, and have our being; as certain also of your own poets have said, For we are also his offspring.

In this sermon to Greek philosophers, Paul did not begin by quoting Scripture but by talking about the first teaching of the Scripture—the divine Creator. This God whom they did not know **made the world and all things therein.** Not only is He the Creator of all things, but He is also **Lord of heaven and earth.** He has not left the good earth He created, but He is the Ruler and Sustainer of the earth and of the people of the earth.

Because of these truths, certain things about worship are true. For one thing, He **dwelleth not in temples made with hands.** In dedicating the temple he had built for the worship of God, Solomon said, "Behold, the heaven and heaven of heavens cannot contain thee; how much less this house that I have builded?" (1 Kings 8:27). Paul also said that the one true God is not **worshiped with men's hands, as though he needed anything.** Nothing that we offer is needed by God for Him to be God. This does not mean that worship does not include giving to God, but it emphasizes that God is not dependent on what people can give to Him. Instead, God is the One who **giveth to all life and breath, and all things. Life** is a gift from God.

When God created people, He **made of one blood all nations. Blood** is not a translation of a word in the Greek text. The Greek text literally reads, "He made of one." Most Bible students believe that Paul was thinking of Adam, the one man from whom all have descended. This common humanity underlies all the differences that have taken place since the creation of one man in God's own image. Although human differences are real, all people share a common humanity.

God has not left people to their own devices. He made humans with freedom of choice, and God is not responsible for the sinful uses of freedom. However, God is not absent from the earth and the people He created. To the contrary, He **hath determined the times before appointed, and the bounds of their habitation** ("the times set for them and the exact places where they should live," NIV). This may be a reference to the regular seasons that the Creator created. However, it probably refers to God moving in the affairs of nations to work out His will. The *New English Bible* reads, "He fixed the epochs of their history and the limits of their territory." "Thus, although God cannot be held responsible for the tyranny or aggression of individual nations, yet both the history and the geography of each nation are ultimately under his control."[3]

God's purpose in creating human beings and moving in the affairs of nations is **that they should seek the Lord, if haply they might feel after him, and find him.** Because people are made by God and for God, our hearts are restless until they rest in Him. God's goal is such a relationship. He has created people and revealed Himself to all people through His creation. Paul added, **Though he be not far from everyone of us.** Even when people have little or no awareness of God, He is near. Actually, God has sought sinful human beings, not we Him.

Rather than quote from the Scriptures, Paul quoted from two Greek poets. First, he cited one line from Epimenides [ehp-ih-MEN-ih-deez] the Cretan (6th century B.C.): **For in him we live, and move, and have our being.** This is surely true and is consistent with biblical teachings. The second poet was Aratus [AR-uh-tuhs], who was influenced by Zeno's Stoic teachings. Referring to Zeus, the chief Greek god, Aratus wrote, **For we are also his offspring.**

Paul's purpose in taking this approach in his message to the Athenian philosophers is consistent with his principle of adjusting his message to his target group. He wrote, "Unto the Jews I became as a Jew, that I might gain the Jews . . . to them that are without law, as without law . . . that I might gain them that are without law . . . I am made all things to all men, that I might by all means save some" (1 Cor. 9:20-22). Missionaries wrestle with this strategy as they try to adapt the good news to a culture different from their own.

Many people in our day believe that missionary work is not needed. Those who study contemporary religions reach different conclusions about the biblical claim that Christ is the only way of salvation (John 14:6; Acts 4:12). Many conclude, "There exists no *one* road to salvation, but many paths—all taking place in different ways within the contexts of the great religious traditions."[4] Paul's words and deeds show that he did not agree. Otherwise he would not have said what he did to the Athenians. These verses show that he believed that other religions show a spiritual hunger, but they do not lead to knowledge of the true and living God.

Why is Jesus the only way? He is the hand of God reaching down to save sinners. All other religions are attempts to reach up to God or to the gods. These assume that people can earn the favor of the gods by something they can do: morality, mysticism, good deeds, and so forth. The Bible says that we are all lost and separated from God, unable to save ourselves by anything we do. Jesus is the only way because what He offers is God's grace for sinners. All the roads leading up the mountain do not reach the top. None of them do. The only way to God is to allow His down-reaching love to save us and lift us up.

People Need to Repent (Acts 17:29-31)

*In what sense are all people **the offspring of God**? What did Paul mean by **the times of this ignorance**? What did he mean by saying that **God winked at** it? What three facts about repentance are in the last part of verse 30? Why did Paul deal with the day of judgment and the resurrection? Why did he not mention the cross?*

Verses 29-31: Forasmuch then as we are the offspring of God, we ought not to think that the Godhead is like unto gold, or silver, or stone, graven by art and man's device. [30]And the times of this ignorance God winked at; but now commandeth all men everywhere to repent: [31]because he hath appointed a day, in the which he will judge the world in righteousness by that man whom he hath ordained; whereof he hath given assurance unto all men, in that he hath raised him from the dead.

Offspring translates *genos,* which means "descendants." In a strict sense, only fellow Christians are considered children of God (by adoption and the new birth). However, all humanity are the offspring of God and sharers of the same humanity. Thus at the very least, all are potentially full children of God. Several conclusions come from the truth that all people are God's offspring. For one thing, **we ought not to think that the Godhead** ("divine being," NIV) **is like unto gold, or silver, or stone, graven by art and man's device.** In other words, idolatry is totally inconsistent with the fact that we are His offspring. The sin of idolatry totally perverts God and human worship of Him. Idols are made and controlled by human beings.

Paul referred to the time before as **times of this ignorance. Ignorance** translates *agnoias,* which is the same basic word as **unknown** (*agnostos*) in verse 23. During the centuries of not knowing the true God, they worshiped false gods. **Winked at** is *huperidon,* which means "overlooked" (NIV, NKJV, HCSB). "The Athenians had good reason, then, to acknowledge their ignorance of God. But, even if such ignorance was not free from blame, God in mercy had passed it over. There is a parallel here not only to the statement in the Lystran speech that in past generations God 'allowed all the nations to go their own ways' (Acts 14:16), but also to Paul's teaching in Rom. 3:25 about God's forbearance in passing over sins committed before the coming of Christ. It is implied in all these places that the coming of Christ marks a fresh start in God's dealings with the human race. . . . If ignorance of the divine nature was culpable before, it is inexcusable now."[5]

The last part of verse 30 makes three points about what God expects in the gospel age. (1) He commands people **to repent.** (2) This is His command to **all men everywhere.** (3) This command is effective **now.** No longer does God overlook any ignorance of Him. All people need to repent of their sins, and they need to do it now. This is a universal command to all people and it urgently needs to be obeyed now. Verse 31 shows that the resurrection of Jesus confirmed the reality of the coming judgment, and this too calls for the urgency of repentance.

These three points emphasize the urgency of the missionary task. Life is short and uncertain. People need to respond to the good news while they can. Christians need to take the good news to all people while yet there is time.

Today missions people speak of "The Last Frontier." These are the people groups who have little or no access to the good news of Jesus. About 30 percent of the world's people are in these people groups. Many of these groups are in countries closed to official missionaries; therefore, new strategies are being used to reach them. Nonresidential missionaries are Christians who are allowed to be in these lands temporally. One of the best ways to reach the people in these countries is through Christians involved with international business interests in such lands. Another way to reach people from these lands is to make contact with those who visit or study in Christian lands where they can be reached with the gospel and then take it back to their own people.

When Paul preached to the Athenian philosophers, there were three kinds of responses. Some of the listeners mocked Paul and his message of resurrection. Others expressed an interest in hearing more at another time. But some believed, including a member of the Areopagus. No missionary work is totally effective. Responses vary from place to place and from time to time. But believers are accountable for telling the good news, and listeners are accountable for how they respond.

❖ *Spiritual Transformations*

Paul sought every opportunity to witness in Athens because he believed that people without Christ are lost. Paul preached the good news to the Athenian philosophers because he felt a sense of debt to share the saving love he had received. Paul told the Athenians of the true God because their religions did not lead them to Him. Paul called the people to repent right then because the day of judgment is coming.

Why should we tell the good news of Jesus? There is a call from outside, based on the fact that those without Christ are lost. There is a call from inside, based on the debt we owe because we have heard the good news and everyone deserves to hear it. There is the call from above, because Christ is the only way of salvation. There is the call from the future, based on the shortness of the time to decide.

How do these four reasons speak to you about your personal witnessing and about your support of missionaries? _____

_____

Which of these four reasons for telling the good news seems most important to you? Why? _____

Prayer of Commitment: Lord, give me a burden for the lost, and help me to do my part in telling the good news.

[1]Stott, *The Spirit, the Church, and the World,* 277.
[2]Charles Colson, *How Now Shall We Live?* 32.
[3]Stott, *The Spirit, the Church, and the World,* 286.
[4]Ebbie Smith, "Contemporary Theology of Religions," in *Missiology,* 417.
[5]Bruce, *The Book of the Acts,* 340.